The Language of Psychosis

PSYCHOANALYTIC CROSSCURRENTS
General Editor: Leo Goldberger

THE LANGUAGE OF PSYCHOSIS

BENT ROSENBAUM
AND
HARLY SONNE

New York University Press
New York and London
1986

Library of Congress Cataloging-in-Publication Data

Rosenbaum, Bent.
    The language of psychosis.

    (Psychoanalytic crosscurrents)
    Translations of: Det er et band der taler.
    Bibliography: p.
    Includes index.
    1. Schizophrenics—Language. 2. Psychoses.
3. Mentally ill—Language. I. Sonne, Harly.
II. Title. III. Series [DNLM: 1. Psychoanalytic
Interpretation. 2. Schizophrenic Language.
WM 203 R8126d]
    RC514.R646813 1986   616.89′8   86-8636
    ISBN 0-8147-7396-6

CONTENTS

FOREWORD

The *Psychoanalytic Crosscurrents* series presents selected books and monographs that reveal the growing intellectual ferment within and across the boundaries of psychoanalysis.

Freud's theories and grand-scale speculative leaps have been found wanting, if not disturbing, from the very beginning and have led to a succession of derisive attacks, shifts in emphasis, revisions, modifications, and extensions. Despite the chronic and, at times, fierce debate that has characterized psychoanalysis, not only as a movement but also as a science, Freud's genius and transformational impact on the twentieth century have never been seriously questioned. Recent psychoanalytic thought has been subjected to dramatic reassessments under the sway of contemporary currents in the history of ideas, philosophy of science, epistemology, structuralism, critical theory, semantics, and semiology as well as in sociobiology, ethology, and neurocognitive science. Not only is Freud's place in intellectual history being meticulously scrutinized, his texts, too, are being carefully read, explicated, and debated within a variety of conceptual frameworks and sociopolitical contexts.

The legacy of Freud is perhaps most notably evident within the narrow confines of psychoanalysis itself, the "impossible profession" that has served as the central platform for the promulgation of official orthodoxy. But Freud's contributions—his original radical thrust—reach far beyond the parochial concerns of the clinican psychoanalyst as clinician. His writings touch on a wealth of issues, crossing traditional boundaries—be they situated in the biological, social, or humanistic spheres—that have profoundly altered our conception of the individual and society.

A rich and flowering literature, falling under the rubric of "applied psychoanalysis," came into being, reached its zenith many decades ago, and then almost vanished. Early contributors to this literature, in addition to Freud himself, came from a wide range of backgrounds both within and outside the medical/psychiatric field, many later became psychoanalysts themselves. These early efforts were characteristically reductionistic in their attempt to extrapolate from psychoanalytic theory (often the purely clinical theory) to explanations of phenomena lying at some distance from the clinical. Over the years, academic psychologists, educators, anthropologists, sociologists, political scientists, philosophers, jurists, literary critics, art historians, artists, and writers, among others (with or without formal psychoanalytic training) have joined in the proliferation of this literature.

The intent of the *Psychoanalytic Crosscurrents* series is to apply psychoanalytic ideas to topics that may lie beyond the narrowly clinical, but its essential conception and scope are quite different. The present series eschews the reductionistic tendency to be found in much traditional "applied psychoanalysis." It acknowledges not only the complexity of psychological phenomena but also the way in which they are embedded in social and scientific contexts that are constantly changing. It calls for a dialectical relationship to earlier theoretical views and conceptions rather than a mechanical repetition of Freud's dated thoughts. The series affirms the fact that contributions to and about psychoanalysis have come from many directions. It is designed as a forum for the multidisciplinary studies that intersect with psychoanalytic thought but without the requirement that psychoanalysis necessarily be the starting point or, indeed, the center focus. The criteria for inclusion in the series are that the work be significantly informed by psychoanalytic thought or that it be aimed at furthering our understanding of psychoanalysis in its broadest meaning as theory, practice, and sociocultural phenomenon; that it be of current topical interest and that it provide the critical reader with contemporary insights; and, above all, that it be high-quality scholarship, free of obsolete dogma, banalization, and empty jargon. The author's professional identity and particular theoretical orientation matters only to the extent that such facts may serve to frame the work for the reader, alerting him or her to inevitable biases of the author.

The Psychoanalytic Crosscurrents Series presents an array of works from the multidisciplinary domain in an attempt to capture the ferment of scholarly activities at the core as well as at the boundaries of psychoanalysis. The books and monographs are from a variety of sources: authors will be psychoanalysts—traditional, neo- and post-Freudian, existential, object-relational, Kohutian, Lacanian, etc.—social scientists with quantitative or qualitative orientations to psychoanalytic data, and scholars from the vast diversity of approaches and interests that make up the humanities. The series entertains work's on critical comparisons of psychoanalytic theories and concepts as well as philosophical examinations of fundamental assumptions and epistemic claims that furnish the base for psychoanalytic hypotheses. It includes studies of psychoanalysis as literature (discourse and narrative theory) as well as the application of psychoanalytic concepts to literary criticism. It will serve as an outlet for psychoanalytic studies of creativity and the arts. Works in the cognitive and the neurosciences will be included to the extent that they address some fundamental psychoanalytic tenet, such as the role of dreaming and other forms of unconscious mental processes.

It should be obvious that an exhaustive enumeration of the types of works that might fit into the *Psychoanalytic Crosscurrents* series is pointless. The studies comprise a lively and growing literature as a unique domain; books of this sort are frequently difficult to classify or catalog. Suffice it to say that the overriding aim of the editor of this series is to serve as a conduit for the identification of the outstanding yield of that emergent literature and to foster its further unhampered growth.

Leo Goldberger
Professor of Psychology
New York University

PREFACE

When someone talks or writes to you and you listen to or read what is being said, something happens inside you. This book is about listening to someone else and examining one's own listening; it is about analyzing speech and writing and tracing the effects that speech has on the listener.

The book deals especially with those instances in which what is said seems to be peculiar, strange, or incomprehensible. Its point of departure is the processes that take place between people who communicate within the context of private and public psychiatric institutions.

Through our efforts to understand the speaking and writing characteristic of people with severe mental disorders, the schizophrenic psychoses, we hope that their peculiar and less comprehensible language will help to explain what happens in more normally functioning speech and writing.

"It's not people speaking, it's a tape." This is how an elderly psychiatric patient explained her relation to her own speech in one of the many interviews on which this book is based. Another patient felt disturbed because "phonetic transcription" had been put into her. Yet a third patient, who felt "at the moment [he] was made in God's image," thought that he was keeping a journal for the Holy Ghost. Common to all of these patients was that the experience of their own speaking and writing was beyond their capacity to control—something that in one way or another seemed to them strange, inexplicable, uncomfortable, exciting, or the like but that always was "outside" themselves. Although these states of mind are by no means always painful for the patients, they are a strain for the patient's families, colleagues, and friends. To persons in these patient's surroundings, it seems that their judgment and self-awareness do not function. Needless to say, these states of mind can preclude meaningful social interaction.

It is generally agreed that these experiences are psychotic states and that people in such states are difficult to treat. In this book we argue that it is possible to investigate and explain the communicative phenomena characteristic of states of psychosis. We also argue for the benefits of psychotherapeutic treatment for people imprisoned in a state of psychosis.

In order to explain the processes that form the bases of psychotic experiences, thoughts, and emotions, we have used statements, letters, diaries, and writings of all kinds that express these states. We have also interviewed a number of people who have been in treatment in various psychiatric institutions for varying lengths of time. We have also used several psychoanalytical, psychiatric, and psychological theories, as well as theories of language and the science of text, all of which, in their own way, contribute to a description of these states. This book demonstrates and explains the theoretical and clinical bases of the problems.

We should like to thank the Danish Medical Research Council and the Danish Research Council for the Humanities for supporting this project.

We would like to thank Margaret Malone and Lene Werdelin for their help in translating this book from the original Danish version (1979). Also we would like to thank the department of psychiatry at the State University Hospital in Copenhagen and Sanct Hans Hospital in Roskilde for their unfailing help and support. Professor Erik Strömgren, Associate Professor Per Aage Brandt, chief psychiatrist Finn Jørgensen, D.M.S.c. Alice Theilgaard and lecturer Christian Grambye supported and stimulated our work in a number of ways. Finally, we would like to thank all the patients who participated in our research.

Copenhagen & Utrecht, 1986

INTRODUCTION

POWER AND KNOWLEDGE IN
THE PSYCHIATRIC INSTITUTION

The letters and interviews reproduced in this book come from people who have been patients in psychiatric institutions. Much of the psychiatric treatment for severe disorders such as schizophrenic psychosis takes place in institutions. Therefore, it seems appropriate to discuss briefly the ways in which the organization of the psychiatric institution affect behavior and language.

Many factors influence and frame the forms of communication, types of treatment, and other activities that take place within psychiatric institutions. In their carefully structured daily rhythm, institutions very often have strict norms with regard to what one may say, think, and feel. The physical layout, the schedule of activities, the hierarchy of power—all affect the way patients are treated. Moreover, the dominant political, ideological, and social conditions affect the nonverbal ways in which individuals are treated.

A small but significant portion of the population spend much of their lives in psychiatric institutions.[1] In Denmark, for example for about three quarters of one percent of the population the psychiatric institution is, to use Goffman's term, "total."[2] It influences the shape and rhythm of their whole existence, whether they are inside or outside the hospital. These persons are almost completely defined by institutional regulations. The technical and scientific level of sophistication of the institution determines their treatment. They are supported and controlled by means of the various methods and products of this technology. As individuals, they are understood, and they are then educated so that they will conform to the norms, rules, and ideology of the institution.

Most psychiatric patients take some form of medication. Chronic schizophrenic patients are thus constantly subject to the effects, and often the side effects of drugs. Both institutional psychiatry and the drug industry take the position that patients "need" drugs in suitable doses. As a matter of fact, the administration of psychopharmacological drugs is often the institution's *only* answer to the patient's mental problems. According to this view, the patient's problems can be solved through psychopharmacological agents without any form of psychotherapeutic intervention. Yet this "nonverbal" form of treatment can be seen, to a certain extent, as a "dialogue." The patient's symptoms constitute a series of questions; drugs represent the answer. Symptoms referred to in the drug industry's advertisements (hallucinations, anxiety, delusions, stereotypical behavior) and their illustration in graphically compelling ways are considered as the patient's message to the therapist. In these advertisements the therapist's answer to the patient is provided in the form of the name of the drug, a list of its properties, and its recommended dosage.

Biological psychiatry goes hand in hand with the drug industry in its domination of the definition and concept of illness. These two entities together decide what is pseudoscience and what can and cannot be done in institutionalized psychiatric treatment.[3] It is our opinion, this situation ought to be changed.

The psychopharmacological dialogue is a very simple exchange of meaning. In our view, its success depends unequivocally upon a patient-therapist relationship of trust and/or submission. It is impossible to include this relationship in the psychopharmacological dialogue's definition of what is taking place. This interaction falls outside the framework of pharmacological science, namely, the language of the relationship itself, or the *textual nature of therapy.* The biologically oriented psychiatrist who advocates drug use may also be aware of other factors influencing the treatment of the patient. Clearly, the treatment situation itself has a suggestive effect on the patient, and the pathological picture can therefore be changed in unexpected and uncontrollable ways. To the pharmacologically oriented psychiatrist, this placebo effect is a side effect of the treatment. Needless to say, biological research is trying to eliminate this factor as much as possible.

Psychopharmacological treatment seldom (or never) deals with the causes of illness. It is exclusively directed toward alleviating symptoms. In the case of schizophrenic psychosis, this treatment is intended to alter the patient's painful, threatening, or anxiety-filled experiences. In our opinion, psychopharmacological products are an inadequate answer to the questions posed by the patient's mental problems. Moreover, treatment with drugs completely conceals the causes of the patient's problems. In contrast to biologically oriented psychiatry, psychotherapeutically oriented research regards the placebo effect as one that is inherent in any treatment. It is merely one of the many effects at work in the treatment. The suggestive effect of the therapeutic dialogue is in no way meaningless from a scientific point of view. It is, on the contrary, very much part of the therapeutic process.

In addition, there are sciences other than the psychobiologically oriented disciplines—those which have text, signification, and subject as their objects of research—in which it is the relation among these that determines what happens between patient and therapist and that we have called the textual nature of therapy.

Language plays an important role in every social situation and affects the very processes that create and regulate our fantasies, thoughts, and feelings. We shall return to this theme many times in this book.

Linguistic, textual, and subjective phenomena cannot be described exclusively by means of biologically oriented psychiatry and its conceptual apparatus. However much speech and thought include the physiological processes of the brain, the mere description of these processes will never lead to an understanding of speech and thought. Sociological and humanistic concepts are needed to attain an understanding.

All persons involved in treatment, whatever their position in the hierarchy, should work both practically and theoretically with the social, linguistic, and intersubjective problems of the conversation process.

The Diagnosis of Psychosis

The letters, interviews, and other, similar quotations in this book are representative of the speaking and writing that take place every day in psychiatric institutions. No doubt any therapist would, without great difficulty, be able to make a tentative diagnosis of the letter writer or the interviewee on the basis of the distinctive features of the texts alone. There are, of course, important differences between written and oral texts. From the diagnostic point of view, however, the similarities are far greater. In the chapters that follow we shall concentrate on these similarities.

If a number of people, chosen at random, were asked to describe these texts, they would probably characterize them as "eccentric," "meaningless," "odd," "incomprehensible," "impossible to identify with," "strange," or "detached from reality." All these expressions point to the texts' lack of normality, their madness. At the same time, as the texts are defined as being deviant in some way or another, the various labels put on them indicate a *place* from which the "deviant" or the "mad person" is regarded as "deviating from" or "deviating away from"—a place that is self-described as "reason," "judgment," or "psychiatry." In fact, all the expressions mentioned are taken from approved psychiatric textbooks.

These descriptive terms are used in different ways in institutionalized psychiatry, depending on intention and aim. But in one way or the other, as a rule they form *the immediate point of departure* for a more technically elaborate diagnosis. The distinctive speech, writing, and whole behavior are, after all, the usual reasons why such persons need psychiatric treatment.

Psychiatry characterizes patients through legal, morally evaluative, and socially descriptive terms. Most psychiatrists believe the schizophrenic psychoses are biologically based.

Yet in the early twentieth century, the beginning of modern psychiatry, authorities in the field warned doctors about unthinkingly turning legal, moral, and socially descriptive terms into psychiatric concepts. They pointed out that there was not necessarily a correspondence between concepts and models of illness in medical science as a whole and psychiatry in particular. "The concept of mental illness (as it is now and as it ought to be) is rather a social than a medical concept," wrote Eugen Bleuler in 1919.[4] And his contemporaries, among them Karl Jaspers and Sigmund Freud, were no less skeptical than Bleuler about references to underlying biological factors ("biological reductionism"). Eventually these warnings were heeded, and so-called multifactorial models of illness are now usually used in modern psychiatry, models that take into account both the biological basis and the social effects of the illness. In spite of this, biological reductionism has maintained its ascendancy in most contemporary schools of psychiatry.

As a result, research in modern clinical psychiatry has had a tendency to dissect and systematize psychopathological symptoms. Accordingly, symptoms are defined psychodynamically or behavioristically and organically. Both types of symptom are empirical: they are seen, measured, or registered with the help of testing devices or laboratory analyses. In addition, observations are systematized in accordance with the research model as defined by the natural sciences. Observations are subjected to statistical analysis as the information from the questionnaires used in the investigation, rating scales, and behavioral tests that are recorded on tape are matched with various psychochemical measurements. Then obstensibly "statistically significant" correlations appear between the psychodynamic or behavioral observations and the psychochemical or psychophysiological observations. The latter are the "reliable" scientific basis of the investigation; the others are included only on the basis of the "reliable" observations.

This research has thus tried to live up to the natural sciences' ideal of objectivity, which is achieved by subordinating the psychological factor and simultaneously reducing the problems of investigations. It is openly admitted that the psychiatric basis of clinical psychiatric research is not yet reliable. Yet, an attempt is made to fulfill the demands of objectivity by eliminating "subjective factors" in the experimental situation, especially those which come from the researcher.

Therefore, it is not only the socially descriptive, legal, and moral characterization of patients in daily psychiatric practice but also the scientific basis of clinical psychiatric research that, in our opinion, should be challenged. Severe mental disorders, the psychoses, should also be analyzed and treated as relations among *language, creation of meaning,* and *subject.* Only by including the fundamental function of speech in the mental life of the human being is it possible to account for processes that cause illness and to indicate possibilities for treating the illness. The French psychoanalyst Jacques Lacan expresses it thus: "The condition of the subject (neurosis or psychosis) is dependent on what is being unfolded in the other [i.e., the generalized impression about somebody else who knows about one]. What is being unfolded there is articulated like a discourse."[5] Lacan emphasizes that the treatment and, indeed, the whole conception of psychosis must of necessity take its point of departure from the way language is used. This is the point of view that we shall try to elaborate on here and throughout this book. On the basis of psychoanalytic and textual theories, we shall regard signification and speech as factors that play a part in the creation of mental disorders and that constitute the scientific basis for analyzing and treating them.

The Limitation of the Problems

The issues discussed in this book are naturally limited. It is not our aim to present a cohesive theory of the individual in society, concepts of illness, or the processes inherent in capitalist society that create illness in individuals. Nor is it our aim to polemicize against the various concepts of psychosis, schizophrenia, and the more general concepts of the relation of the speaking individual to language that directly or indirectly, are debated here and in the chapters that follow. Instead, we have tried to treat the problems pragmatically in such a way that the different models we sketch indicate where and in what way one can analyze and "place oneself" in relation to the way schizophrenics see the world. When we deal with various aspects of the problems, we may appear to reduce the whole from which the problems have emerged and appear as problems. This is nonetheless the case in connection with concepts like psychosis and schizophrenia. We do not take into account questions, for example, of how the *causes* of psychosis and schizophrenia can be described or to what extent the concepts of psychosis and schizophrenia will be radically changed or even disappear in postrevolutionary, socialist societies with other family structures. What we try to describe is *the reality of schizophrenia* and *the subject's relation to reality through language*.

As we have indicated, our point of departure has been the expressions of schizophrenia present in the patients' letters, notes, diaries, and written requests we have collected. In addition, we have videotaped a number of interviews and tape-recorded a number of informal conversations with patients in psychiatric institutions. The date of this material has naturally varied. Many of the letters were written in the beginning of the century, some even before 1900. This difference in time and historical context has presented us with certain methodological problems, especially when reading the older texts. In order to avoid mistakes in reading, or misunderstandings, we have tried to take into account information from the patients' files, even though this is not apparent in our analyses. Many hospital files from the period before 1910 contain extremely accurate and detailed descriptions of patients' behavior, language, and experiences. Therefore, even if the analyses may appear to be "isolated" or "autonomous," there is material that lends further support to our claims in almost every case. As a matter of principle we have decided not to publish this background material.

In the case of the states of schizophrenia, there are obviously some differences with regard to time, class, sex, and age and, more generally, with respect to society and culture. However, as far as we can judge at the present time, there is little indication that these differences are of *decisive* importance when analyzing the reality of schizophrenia.[6] On the contrary, we have been struck by the similarities between texts from the 1890s and texts and interviews from the 1970s, when historically specific ideas and values are ignored. In the 1890s many patients spoke about "magnetism;" in the 1970s, about "radioactivity." The 1890 texts are frequently adressed to royalty; the 1970 texts, to the parliamentary ombudsman or the CIA.

The book is structured in the following manner. In Chapter 2 we present the method of reading we employ in connection with a tentative definition of the relations among language, signification, and subject. In Chapters 3 and 4 we present some of the observable changes in text production that characterize states of schizophrenia. This is primarily a case of the speech's presentation of its "place of origin" and the presentation of the "receiver" or "receivers" of the speech that every text contains. It is, furthermore, a case of the way in which the speech or text presents time, place, and subject matter, a presentation that seems decisively altered in schizophrenia. In the next two chapters (5 and 6) we argue that this "place of speech" is due to a specific organization of the body as mental representation, and we try to illustrate the connection between body representation and speech by analyzing the way in which the fantasy enters into the construction of the state of schizophrenia. In the penultimate chapter (7), we describe the forms of criticism of the surroundings, especially, of course, of the exercise of authority that takes place in psychiatric institutions, which many of the texts are about. Finally, in Chapter 8 we attempt to sketch some of the therapeutic consequences for treatment implied by the theoretical and analytical points of view.

CHAPTER ONE
"IT'S A TAPE THAT'S SPEAKING"

EXCERPTS FROM AN INTERVIEW[1]

1

I. Is it something you have experienced?

P. No, yes, it's been said to us.

I. Aha.

P. Yes, it's been said.

I. Who said it to you?

P. Well, I can hardly remember who. There are many young gentlemen here, many young people who have been separated, and they have said it—they have told something about it. Yes.

I. Where are these young people?

P. Well, they are three hundred things after all, so we are, we had people all over space, yes. There were . . . the whole of space was filled with people and then they were put into three skins at our place. [Three skins (*tre hamme*): in Nordic mythology, when an individual puts on a skin, he or she changes character at the same time.]

I. Three skins?

P. Yes, they were put into the body, but I think that two of the skins are ready, they should be ready, they should be separated. And there were three hundred thousand who had no reason, or soul, or reason. But now they are so . . . , now it seems that there are some who have neither soul nor reason and they had to be helped, and people have to be helped, I can't do it here in this where we are, we have to be in . . . if I am to take care of these things. These . . . that's what the ladies say, they are aware . . .

I. Oh, you are saying that you can't help the people where you are?

P. Yes.

I. Do you mean that you can't help the people while you are in hospital?

P. No, I can't. I can't. Because one can't speak, so I can't . . . must be helped, they must be helped in various ways. I can't. No.

I. In what ways do you help these people?

P. Well, I can't—I can't say it. I don't really want to say it. If anyone is listening to this then I don't really want to say it.

I. Hm.

P. Yes.

I. Is that a secret way then?

P. No, it isn't. It's a very useful way. That's the way I've helped them in Øster Søgade [a street in Copenhagen] we helped them in that way.

I. In Øster Søgade?

P. Yes, we helped them in that way there and there were many who slid away and many who were helped. Yes.

I. There were many who slid away and many who were helped?

P. Yes, I don't know how many, I don't know. But there are many trisks and svilts [patient's neologisms] and people, there are people and trisks and svilts. I think there are most trisks and svilts. That is those who are made out of svilt clay.

I. Out of svilt clay?

P. Yes, It is out on space. They make them in trilms [patient's neologism].

I. Trilm?

P. By trilms. And then they go through three levels. Some only go through two. Some go through three. Yes. When they make them.

I. Is svilt clay something I can touch?

P. Yes, I don't know, it's something that's made, that's made out of dogs who were dead, they have lain bodily out in the spaces. They all wanted to have a relationship with . . . with everything they came near. And they follow those. . . . They, ah, they follow those who are made out of svilt clay. They always want a sexual relationship . . .

I. They want a sexual relationship?

P. Yes, they want a sexual relationship. Precisely. Some go . . . perhaps don't have so much with that . . . they want to interfere and destroy everything . . . yes . . . I don't know if there is anyone who is listening to this. It's not certain they can understand it.

I. Do you think they can't understand it?

P. No. I don't know if they can understand it, those who are listening to this.

I. Would you like people to . . . to understand it?

P. Well, not when I'm in this place. We can't, otherwise we would, it's very good that people understand it. Many people in Copenhagen understand it and they've listened to . . . we . . . we have a tape that speaks. It's a *tape* speaking now [English "tape" = Danish *bånd*].

I. It's a *child* that's speaking now? [English "child" = Danish *barn*]

P. Yes, because our, um, our, um people, the two vicars' wives, they don't speak very much, and therefore it's an old tape speaking.

I. It's an old tape speaking?

P. It's an old tape speaking when . . .

I. When you are speaking now?

P. Yes, that's a tape too. And it's an old skin, I don't know, it's been so abused, we're sitting in, on the vicars' wives.

2

I. Could I also go and see it if I wanted to?

P. Yes, that is if you have perspectives. And see it, then you can see it down under Øster Søgade.

I. Could anybody see it?

P. Anyone who has perspectives *can* see it.

I. Anyone who has perspectives . . . ?

P. And *can* see . . .

I. And *can* see . . . ?

P. Yes.

I. Even when you *yourself* haven't seen it?

P. Yes.

I. When did you . . . did you read . . . ?

P. No, it's a tape, it's a tape that's speaking, yes, it's a tape that's speaking, that's been recorded.

I. Aha.

P. We have lots of things that are recorded on the tape. And, um, they are correct things. One can investigate that.

I. This tape. Is it something inside of you or is it something that has to do with . . .

P. Well, it's in the vicar's wives, it has slide in, it has slid in, it's been in a skin, in the words, but most people are separated here, there have been a lot of people. And there have been large blocks which slid out yesterday, large blocks of people who were blocked together. They . . . we let them slide out into the sugar pools.

I. Out into the sugar pools?

P. Yes, the sugar pools, yes. Then they are dissolved and they can exist better.

I. Doesn't that sound pretty grim?

P. Yes, it does, but one can investigate and see if it's true.

3

I. Um, at home, do you sit and think about these things, or what do you do at home?

P. Well, now they've got *Berlingske Tidende* [a conservative daily newspaper], so I read *Berlingske Tidende* aloud. There are twenty [Danish *tyve* can mean either "thieves" or "twenty"] from different planets who listen to it, and one from this planet who listens to it, and if there is anything which must . . . can be helped through the newspapers, I can't see what it is, but they know what it is, and if there is anything there machines or children or anything which should be helped . . .

I. Who can see it?

P. It, they, those who listen from different planets, there are twenty or maybe more who listen from different planets, perhaps there are some from different, what shall I say, departments or trisks and svilts and to people, and there is also someone from this planet who listens, yes. And so I read the newspaper aloud when I get the opportunity. Or, read aloud or show them the pages and they have to look for themselves because I can't see . . .

I. Can you talk to these trisks and svilts?

P. Well, they don't speak to anyone. But a wire can be attached to them, then they're able to speak.

I. Hm. Have you attached . . . ?

P. People have been put into them. Then they can speak.

I. Hm.

P. No, I don't speak with them. We're not allowed to speak very much. A tape explains it to us.

I. Hm. That means that you don't think you are speaking your-self? It's a tape that's speaking?

P. Yes, it's a tape that's speaking.

I. Hm.

P. There isn't anything that . . . it's not people speaking. It's a tape that's like in the Parliament, there they also have, I don't know who, they have tapes there too. They talk . . .

I. They have tapes in the Parliament?

P. Yes, there . . . they have tapes they talk on. But it's the same, you know, trisks and svilts, you know, it's the same, when one has tapes, it's the same.

I. Oh . . .

P. Yes, they don't really care when one has tapes. They don't pay any attention to that.

TWO LETTERS²

1

Date 27th November 19—

The American Police

2 idiots Frederik the 7th and Christian P., son of Valborg R. 2 t Sankt Hans are the reason they breathe shamelessly on me Miss Valborg R. and on C Mrs. S. F.

When I say one thing, that the 2 idiots *Must Drink Murder* for nothing then that is *my* opinion. Not that they are to be A Total Insanity to their acquaintances as nurse.

It is she Valborg R., who has also given birth to N. N. [the patient's name], who is against the freedom of the world.

She is *Not* to be found. She can just shit and breathe me during the day, and at night also into the mouth. But I shall bloody well get her to drink the murders off with a hundred years rejection from America. When Africa has been cleared of animals then it is there. Australia must also be cleared. The *decadences* are to go in and *all All All Murders* to be drunk off. 54 millions in *decadences* and Wild *Peoples*. The English may get Copenhagen. for decadences and wild peoples. Europe pulls out. Africa pulls out. Asia pulls out. Want to be murdered English for *wanting* to come in from the Earth. Clean up in the grass so the rats are not there. like Africa. No animals in America. No animals in Africa. No animals in Europe. No animals. No radio N. N. daughter of Frederik the 7th No millions.

N. N.

2

Berlin's and Madrid's Police
Berlin

6th November 19—

Mr. J. N.
Sankt Hans
About clothes, then 46 and 48 are nightdresses for women which are usable. No smaller sizes. Dresses as well. Forbidden of cotton clothes, but of heavy like German. Dress makosan shirt, chemise, *Warm Trousers*, not the other, slip, narrow of makosan, stockings and good slippers. *Belt* sewn on. 2 buttons for wide and tight. Dresses not 3 inches—but a single old dress becomes small. must not be stocked. 0 and 1 *dresses not*
Coffee serving in bed otherwise according to American system, Rio de Joneiro. Up 10–2. Knitting and other work trained.
Discharge. *Must* drink murder off. Abortion *Skinning*. Decadence. I do not want prisoners or patients. One piece in the evening or as American. Good *food* for dinner *lovely* potatoes *sauce* almost none. Vegetables. Blood pudding canceled milk and scones, kedgeree and salt herring canceled, and semolina no milk in the bread pudding.
Porridge no spread rice flour just all right beer. The coffee and the food are prepared according to the American. Knit refreshments and the face-cloth's. No supplementary but American. No plant pots. Peat shed. for dwelling stove. About the baths, then water in lower. The ears thought on with brush. Dissolution of some kind or other. Nails cut close close.

N. N.

CHAPTER TWO

THE OTHER IN SPEECH

A STRATIFICATION OF TEXT

In textual analysis we see no reason to distinguish between written and spoken texts. This approach applies equally to texts produced by psychotic patients. Written and spoken texts, of course, do differ in many respects. The spoken language and accompanying gestures, can seem more freely expressive but are, at the same time, more tied to the specific situation. Written texts can appear less bound to a situation where the conversation partner is actually present. Yet they are more tied to genre, frequently composed in accordance with rules appropriate to written messages of the type in question (complaint, personal letter, contribution to a debate, outburst of anger, apology, polite correction) and determined by the institution where the communication is uttered.

Nonetheless, spoken and written texts share many important features. They are all *stratified*; that is, they contain several different but interdependent levels that correspond to different aspects of the dimensions of the text. We shall first briefly describe these four levels and then present the model of textual analysis that we shall use to describe the communication of schizophrenic patients.

1. Each text is about something: it points out, names and presents some matter, or it deals with a topic, an object, or human beings and their conditions and relations.

2. As the text progresses it moves from one topic to another or from one part of the topic to another. This progression can be looked at in two ways; in part as a movement in time and in part as a logical sequence.

3. In the context of these two elementary levels—that is, subject matter and narrative—a speaking figure, a "sender," is being presented in the text. This is the point of communication from which the subject matter and its narrative are presented. This sender communicates with a participant who is known beforehand and calculated into the communication—a "receiver." Texts are thus basically dialogic. The speaker addresses a questioner who is present, at least always present *in the text*. In this way the text presents a *certain relationship between the speaker and the other to whom the text is adressed.*

4. When we look at the text as a whole, we see that by means of these three levels a textual reality is presented that includes both the subject matter of the text and the relationship that the speaker expresses toward the other, the person spoken to. The text's presentation of reality constitutes the fourth level in the stratification. Here the relation to (similarity to, or difference from) other texts is decisive. On this last level the text can be regarded as part of a greater whole, a "thinking," an ideology with appropriate media and genres, whose rules determine the actual formation of the text.

Let us illustrate this stratification with a short text written by a schizophrenic patient.

> The burning question of today is the proposal put by the conspirators which is about removing all things living and dead between Heaven and Earth. In this way they think that they will be able to make room for something new and better, which is supposed to come out of the rays of the sun. However, I shall apply for permission to form an exception.[1]

In this text the subject matter is twofold: the end of the world and the wish to escape if it comes. One subject is replaced by another in such a way that the time sequence in the text is organized first around "the end of the world" and then around the "I," who thus regards himself as sharing the fate of the world. The first topic logically forms a clear basis for the second. It proves more difficult to find clear and stable features of the relationship between the sender and the receiver. The patient who is writing the letter is present in the form of an "I," but where is the receiver in relation to this "I"? Who might answer this request? On this point the text is unclear, and this is an important reason why the reality it represents must seem more or less impenetrable. The whole that regulates the text—the other texts that it should be possible to compare with—is unknown. We are now in a position to give a brief description of our operational model of textual analysis, which corresponds to the four levels of the text:

1. The subject matter is produced as certain themes that belong together semantically or that delimit themselves in relation to one another, for example in contradictory relationships or relationships of repetition or parallelism. The themes may be defined in terms of similarity and proximity between semantic units. *Thematic analysis* deals with the interconnection and the logical relation of themes; for example, in the schizophrenic text quoted above, the relations among semantic units such as life, death, old, new, known, unknown, and their semantic relations and coherence are considered.[2]

2. The progression of the text is presented in accordance with ideologically inscribed preformed series in the form of logical (con)sequences, chains of conclusion, canonized orders of presentation and narrative method, which help to produce the coherence of the text and thus make it understandable in the same way as in its thematic organization. Thus, *narrative analysis* deals with themes sequentially and logically distributed.[3]

3. *Enunciation analysis* investigates all those elements and conditions that, on the one hand, help to produce the combined effect that we have called the sender of the text, and, on the other hand, help to produce the relationship between the speaker and the other.[4] In psychiatric literature, the communicative contact of

schizophrenic communication is often characterized as being weakened or nonexistent. This is due to the deviant, peculiar character of the enunciation of schizophrenic texts. Enunciation analysis concentrates on who says what is being said, on the speaker's relationship to what is being said, and on his or her relationship to the implied receiver, whether or not the latter is present in the conversation situation. From the short text we have looked at, it can be established that the enunciation of schizophrenic texts is remarkable when compared with everyday written and oral communications as here, an application addressed to a public authority. In the schizophrenic text "the conspirators" are mentioned, and although they are not identified, it must really be them to whom the text is addressed.

4. The text as a total expression of the speaker's conception of reality, *its presentation of reality*, is investigated and identified by means of *discourse analysis*.[5] We call this discourse analysis rather than, for example, analysis of reality, because the text's presentation of reality is always a question of its relation to other texts, its *intertextuality*. Intertextuality is historically determined. What it is possible and reasonable to say in a given society at a given time may in another society at another time be an expression of "madness." In medieval times the text we quoted could very well have been meaningful and could have been regarded as a reasonable utterance when compared with, for example, prophetic religious texts produced in that society. However, the intertextuality of this text is different in modern middle-class society.

The text's presentation of reality depends on its relation to other texts. Such relations are called *discursive relations*. The concept of discourse includes linguistic entities, systematic bodies of text, greater than the individual text that decides its formation and function. We can distinguish several discourses behind the brief wording in the letter by the schizophrenic patient. There is partly the religious and literary discourse that marks the choice of words, "all things living and dead between Heaven and Earth," and partly a kind of political discourse seen in expressions like "the burning question of today," "the conspirators," "permission to form an exception." The textually produced reality is at the same time global or universal and local or particular. This concurrent duality of reality (global-local) is one of the characteristics we shall examine more closely in the following chapters.

Analytically, the text is thus organized on four levels: *theme, narrative, enunciation*, and *discourse*. In our opinion, the production of texts, understood as the actual, physically manifested formation of sentences and text, should not be analyzed only according to the rules that organize the levels separately. In reality, texts are produced in the following way. Briefly, the process starts with the formation of syllables and words (which we do not include in our levels of textual analysis). It then proceeds to a thematic and narrative organization of words and sentences right up to the levels of enunciation and discourse. Enunciation and discourse operate not only on the level of the individual sentence but also on the level of sentence relations in which the sentences *presuppose, refer to, and repeat* each other. At the same time, enunciation and discourse refer *back* to the first phases of the process. The complex levels influence the elementary levels. This means, for example, that the relationship between sender and receiver in the enunciation is quite decisive for the formation of syllables and words on the elementary levels too. This is not least the case in such unpleasant situations as a driving test or an examination. Think, for example, of the way the candidate stutters and stammers when faced with the implied receivers, the examiner and the external examiner, and in relation to the discourse that he or she has to repeat, criticize, and so on.

It is seldom very difficult to describe and identify the first two analytical levels of texts produced by schizophrenic patients. Theme and narrative in schizophrenic texts can seem so deviant and meaningless, incoherent and astonishing that psychiatric textbooks can describe them in terms such as "word salad." In the above example, the sense, content, or meaning of the text may seem veiled and unclear when compared with "normal" communication. But the analysis of theme and narrative does not present any real problems. Later on, we shall focus on theme, partly with an eye to the references in the contents to the speaker's body and the world around him or her. At this point, we shall examine the difficulties often met with when we have to relate theme and narrative in schizophrenic texts to their enunciation and discourse, that is, when we analyze the relationship between subject matter and progression on the one hand and between sender and receiver on the other. It is precisely this relationship that is essential to the analysis of the conceptual universe expressed in the content of the thematic and narrative elements, for example, in the "fables," structured tales of a consistent nature, which schizophrenic patients can spend a lot of their time producing.

In the linguistic production of schizophrenic patients, the relationship between theme/narrative and enunciation/discourse is crucial. As mentioned in the Introduction, Lacan regards language—the workings of linguistic production in the socially determined individual—as the process through which the individual achieves an identity and becomes an individual.[6] "We must point out that however much language may consist of bla bla bla, it is from this that any having and being emanate." Later on, Lacan specifies this "bla bla bla" by means of stratification not unlike the one we are working with here. He emphasizes that "what the unconscious presents for our examination is a law whereby enunciation will never be able to be reduced to the proposition of any speech." We regard the *proposition* in speech as its thematic and narrative content and meaning or, in other words, what the text is about. Lacan, however, stresses precisely the significance of enunciation, a significance that is no less important when analyzing the language and subjectivity of schizophrenic patients.

Because of the central position of enunciation, we shall briefly describe the concepts of enunciation analysis that we regard as essential in connection with the questions raised by the distinctive features of schizophrenia. Subsequently we shall formulate some of the relations between enunciation and discourse that form the basis of our theory about the communication of schizophrenic patients.

ENUNCIATION AND DISCOURSE

The originator of the text, its prime mover, is its *First Person*. However, the production of text—spoken or written—is everywhere subject to certain necessary conditions: it takes place in time and space and vis-à-vis *another person* who may be present or absent (existing in the situation or "internalized"). This other person, then, is either in fact listening or reading or has been integrated into the speaking or writing individual, as when someone is writing or mumbling in solitude. Since the production of texts is subject to all these conditions, it follows that all the elements in the text that indicate or refer to the condition can be understood as a receiver built into the text, its *Second Person*.

As distinct from these two is the third element, what is being talked about in the text, regardless of whether it has to do with absent or present, existent or nonexistent things, persons, circumstances, matters, or the like. In grammatical descriptions of language, this third element in the text is categorized as its *Third Person*.

The sender, the First Person, organizes his message by presenting the proposition, that is, the Third-Person elements in such a way that the receiver, the Second Person, will be able to *see*, that is, visualize or picture to himself what is being said in the text. The way in which the Second Person comes to perceive the narrative and thematic elements of the text is determined by a number of factors. Among them are the factors that in the philosophy of language and linguistics are termed "speech acts," and those factors which are categorized together as modalities. Speech acts are linguistic expressions that have institutionalized validity as social acts (e.g., a promise, a judgment, some advice). Modalities are words, phrases, and verb forms, indicating whether the sender wants to influence the receiver so as to make him or her perceive the subject matter as, for example, real or imagined, possible or impossible, probable or improbable. The sentences "There ought to be more bicycle paths"; "It is a sure thing", "It's raining"; "It will probably be raining tomorrow as well" all indicate in different ways how the sender relates to his topic and thus indicate the sender's influence on the Second Person with regard to this topic.

Explicitly or implicitly, all sentences contain a structure in which an *I* "says" that a *you* must "see" that *this* is (perhaps/certainly/not at all, etc.) the case (see Table 2.1). This table is the basic enunciation structure of the text. One essential function maintained by this enunciation structure is that, built into any text, there is a presupposed scale or standard in the form of I / You / Here / Now systems relating to time and place or space. Time, place, persons, and subject matter are always measured according to such a stable system, whether it is explicitly expressed in the actual wording of the sentences or just implicitly there, operating unseen in the enunciation structure. For example, the sentence "It comes tomorrow"[7] can be understood only in relation to some previously established order dependent on the workings of the I / You / Here / Now system. "It" must have been defined in advance (as a letter, a TV program, a thunderstorm, or something else), through what has been said before, or through "it" being pointed out before the eyes of a Second Person actually present (e.g., see what is said below about anaphora and deixis). Comes—meaning "will come"—implies a future in relation to the present marked out by the speech, that is, the Now of the I / You / Here / Now system. Moreover, "comes" implies a place to which something comes, a place that has, like the entity "it," been identified beforehand either through past (or future) speech or by being pointed out. Often the word "come" is used in reference to either the place in which the First

Table 2.1. Simple enunciation

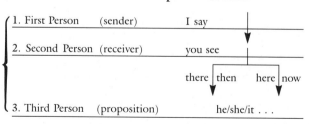

1. First Person	(sender)	I say
2. Second Person	(receiver)	you see
		there ǀ then here ǀ now
3. Third Person	(proposition)	he/she/it . . .

Person or the Second Person or possibly both, are at the moment the sentence is spoken or are going to be later—that is to say, either a Here or a There, again measured according to the presupposed scale of the I / You / Here / Now system. Finally, the sentence "It comes tomorrow" is understood in terms of time, the expression "tomorrow" meaning "the day after today," where once more "today" can be defined only in relation to the moment when the sentence is spoken. This moment of speech, however, is everywhere defined as being the moment, the Now when the implied I/You relation exists, that is, once more the I / You / Here / Now system.

Through the relations between the First, Second, and Third Persons in the enunciation structure of a given text, the text is endowed with a number of characteristic effects. Normally the relationship between the First and Second Persons in the text requires that the First Person be represented as the same identical instance throughout significant portions of the text. If the First Person changes constantly, relations become blurred, there appears to be "speaking in tongues," or the message seems disjointed and incoherent. Any shift in the First Person must, at any rate in principle, be marked in the text. These markings may be in the form of explicit indications that there are other senders ("He had the idea that . . . "; "Of course, many people say that . . . "; "*The Times* writes that . . . "); but more generally these take the form of quotation marks indicating the Second Person that the statement of the First Person should rightly be attributed to another First Person than the one responsible for the text as a whole. This form is used, among other things, in irony.

Through the marking of quotations, there is a more or less explicit *anchoring* of the text, by virtue of which it becomes possible to attribute the different portions of the text to a stable instance. This instance is, on the one hand, responsible for certain parts of the text (without marked quotations) and, on the other hand, *administers the quotations*, those parts of the text for which it is not responsible but for which other instances are senders. The marking of quotations can also take the form of a sort of acting, playing a part, in which by means of vocal pitch, body gesture, and accentuation—and, in the case of written texts, quotation marks—the speaker indicates another sender to whom the text should temporarily be ascribed. Furthermore, the anchoring of the text also has a body aspect, something that is fundamental to the analysis of schizophrenic text production. As will be shown, the body aspect has, to a very large extent, to do with the anchoring of the text, including changes in schizophrenic communication. Even though the text may, on a number of other points, be extremely well adjusted to traditional linguistic standards—grammatical rules may be largely complied with, syntax and orthography may be flawless—it is nevertheless striking that it is precisely its enunciation structure that seems to be in disarray. Of course, this applies also to the relationship to the Second Person and to the relations between the time and space of the text, on the one hand, and on the other, to the actual instances, persons, institutions, powers, and time to which it refers; once again, see the short schizophrenic text considered above. The unreasonableness of the schizophrenic's ideas is due to the fact that their anchoring to the situation of speaking or writing with its time, space, persons, and so on is unstable and not marked in the text. (See Figure 2.1).

At this point we can sum up as follows: the text and its component parts are anchored in two ways. First, they are anchored to the speaking individual represented by the First-Person forms in the explicit or implicit enunciation structure of the text. Second, they are anchored to the stock of texts that the speaker (or writer)

Figure 2.1. Letter sent to Maribo Cathedral, Lolland

Maribo Cathedral
Lolland

19 November 19——

You are kindly requested to remove any obstacles that might exist to the procurement of my liberty.

$$1.12815214 \times 1.12815214 \times 0.7857143 = \underline{1}$$
$$112.81524 \times 112.81524 \times {}^{11}\!/_{14} \times 100 = \underline{1,000,000}$$

[signature]

has at his disposal and from which he may quote. The general intelligibility of the text, including its thematic and narrative purport (meaning, content), is built on a stable and well-functioning anchoring system. In linguistics this system of anchoring and reference functions is called *deixis* (from Greek "pointing to," "referring to"). With this term, many linguists seek to distinguish between anchoring in, and reference to, the time, space, and persons of the enunciation and references to an underlying discourse or "truth" not bound to any particular situation. This "truth" may be more or less generally recognized as being logical, sensible, and so forth under the given circumstances.

Let us consider two examples.[8] In the first example (labeled A), note that,

> A. A horse is a four legged mammal.
>   Århus is the capital of Denmark. [Århus is Denmark's second largest city, the capital is Copenhagen.]
>   Freud died on September 23, 1939.
>
> B. It snowed this morning.
>   No Parking.
>   Here I am.

In the A sentences it is possible to carry out a sort of truth test: they are either right or wrong, true or false. Their veracity does not depend on who utters them, or where or when they are uttered. In the B sentences no such truth test is possible: their truth or falsity depends on the situation in which they are uttered and on the person by whom they are uttered. They are, unlike the A sentences, dependent on who, where, and when. The veracity of the B sentences is relative. Their truth can be determined only by assigning to them the elements of time, space, and person inherent in the situation in which they are uttered. In other words, one must read these sentences in light of their anchorage. Both the A sentences and the B sentences are acceptable and grammatically correct even though one of them is less true than the others. But there is a crucial difference between the two sets of sentences. The difference consists in the two fundamentally different ways in which they are anchored. The B sentences are anchored clearly in time and place; the sentence "No Parking" means only, of course, that vehicles must not be parked at or around the sign that carries the prohibition. It does not apply everywhere. The placing of the sign in time and space thus constitutes the real anchoring of the sentence in and connected to, reality. Unlike the B sentences, the A sentences lack such anchorage. They are general; in terms of time and place they have considerable range and validity, and anybody can utter them. They are actually bound only to a sort of social and cultural common sense—which may, however, be limited in several respects. Other cultures may, for example, employ a different calendar from the one to which "Freud died on September 23, 1939," is anchored. This sentence would, of course, be anchored differently in the discourse of this other culture. The A sentences can be characterized as possessing a truth bound to logic (common sense). The B sentences are rather bound to the speaker or writer, bound to the time, place, and persons of a specific situation, and thus have strong deictic markings.

As we have said before, in everyday text production relatively stable and explicit anchoring systems, or I / You / Here / Now systems, are maintained throughout. The stability and clarity of these systems appears either from the lexical wording of the texts or from the situation that those engaged in the conversation are part of. There are, of course, a multitude of borderline situations where the speakers suddenly perceive that the anchorage of the text has become blurred and confusing. This is the case when two persons are speaking over the telephone and one of them asks the other to get a book in the bookcase. "Just find the one, you know, the one about the Social Welfare Act, it's above, 'em—if you stand with your back to the window it's to the right of. . . ." Oral conversation normally requires both parties to be present in the same room at the same time. That is not the case here, so the text suddenly has to be anchored lexically without being bound to place or gesture (after all, one cannot point over the telephone).

We use the term "deixis" as a comprehensive concept about textual anchorage. Greek and Roman rhetors (teachers of oratory) used deixis to describe a number of linguistic reference functions that could be employed in various stylistically refined ways. But it is only in modern linguistics that deixis has been the object of thorough investigation. The American linguist Charles Fillmore defined "deixis" as lexical items and grammatical forms that can be interpreted only when the sentence they occur in is perceived to be anchored to some social context.[9] The following factors determine the social context: the persons who are engaged in communicating or are part of the speaking situation must have been identified mutually, and their position in time and space relative to the communicative act must have been established. On this basis Fillmore thinks he can distinguish between five different but interrelated types of deixis: deixis providing orientation in space; deixis indicating time; social deixis, which includes deixis "of person"; and finally anaphoric deixis, which points out and refers to elements within the framework of the text itself.

These types of deixis can be expressed lexically or performed by gesture, and they all have the function of anchoring the chain of speech to the social space, the space created by speech, or some generally recognized logical space as indicated above with regard to the A sentences. Moreover, all the spaces directly or indirectly presuppose a prior identification of time, place, parties to the conversation, and mutual relations of the latter. The worst imaginable, totally unanchored text that Fillmore can think of is a small slip of paper found inside a bottle floating in the middle of the Pacific:

MEET ME HERE AT NOON TOMORROW WITH A SMALL STICK ABOUT THIS SIZE IN ONE HAND!

Fillmore distinguishes among different ways of using deixis. We have already mentioned some of these differences. We compared a telephone conversation with a conversation where both parties are present in the same room at the same time. In the latter case, it is possible and common to use *gestural deixis*: "Just give me that, would you," followed by a pointing at, or a nod in, the direction of the desired object. The telephone conversation in the foregoing example rendered gestural deixis unintelligible, and it was necessary to convert it to *symbolic deixis:* "If you stand with your back to the window it's to the right of . . . ." In symbolic deixis, the Second Person's space is referred to only vaguely if at all: "Are you there?" we may ask on the telephone without having to point to the place implied by the deictic "there." *Anaphoric deixis* refers exclusively to elements and relations within the framework of the text itself: "I drove to the car park and parked there," meaning "in the car park," is a previously mentioned element or relation within the framework of the text itself. Anaphoric deixis is also used about elements pointing forward in the text: "The crime was committed exactly where *The Times* had positioned its photographer." It is important to emphasize that these three *forms* of deixis (gestural, symbolic, and anaphoric) functionally stretch far beyond the individual sentence and that the same is true of the different *types* of deixis (temporal, spatial, social, personal, and anaphoric). Finally, it should be noted that anaphoric deixis represents both *type and form*: with regard to content it has the function of pointing to elements within the framework of the text itself, and it constitutes a use of deixis that is limited by this framework.

In language learning, anaphoric deixis is the last form of deixis that a child will acquire. Fillmore relates some experiments with children who are as yet unable to master the fully developed use of deixis. These experiments show that anaphoric deixis is, indeed, by far the most difficult type to administer. In a research laboratory two children were placed on either side of a partition. They were then given a generous supply of building blocks, and each was asked to build a castle out of the blocks. One child was given the building instructions in the form of a drawing of the desired castle and was to give instructions to the other child on the other side of the partition. The exchange of information took place in the following way: "Then you take that block and put it on top of the other one, like this, and then you just have to take one of these and put it crosswise on top of that one, like this, and then . . . ." This is a use of deixis that is exclusively symbolic-gestural, not anaphoric. In other words, the child giving architectural guidance assumes that the Second Person—the other child—is present in the concrete space of reality as well as being present in the space of speech (which corresponds to the space of the telephone conversation in the foregoing example.

The experiment was a great success—even though it yielded two entirely different castles! Evidently the child receiving the instructions worked on the same premises as the child giving them: that the space of speech (anaphoric in kind) was congruent with the space of reality (gestural-symbolic in kind). But the experiment demonstrates clearly that the actual process through which a child learns to pass from the narrowly deictic (gestural and in part symbolic) space bound to persons to the more abstract, anaphoric space bound to speech is a rather difficult process in the learning of language. Later on, we shall consider the text production of schizophrenic patients from these aspects, but we may mention briefly here that for schizophrenic patients there are difficulties when it comes to administering the different forms of deixis.

The administration of deixis—anaphoric deixis in particular—is crucial for the speaker's reason and judgment in relation to the implied Second Person in the enunciation. As we have said, all the points of anchorage in the text and its internal structures of reference constitute an important part of the text's enunciation structure, both its organizing I / You / Here / Now system and the coherence of the presentation of the subject matter (the Third-Person level in the text). Later we shall give a more detailed account of the way in which the basic structure of enunciation is maintained and functions in relation to the speaker and the speaker's conscious or unconscious perception of his or her body as the point of anchorage of his or her speech. For the moment, we can conclude that the space of reality is organized by the speaker's bodily presence and by its linguistic representation. Further, the space of reality is usually marked by a *strong* deixis (gestural and possibly symbolic deixis). The space of speech is marked by a *weak* deixis (predominantly anaphoric but also symbolic deixis). Finally, we may compare these dependent forms of linguistic communication with nondependent forms (see the example with the two sets of sentences, A and B). There, it is not possible to find explicit references to I / You / Here / Now systems; and references have a general quality; they are significative apparently regardless of time, place, persons, and social situations. We placed such sentences in a *logical* space.

The types and the use (forms) of deixis are strongest in the space of reality and weakest in the logical space. In the space of reality the body is connected directly with the speech or, to put it more generally, with the text. In contrast, the space of speech connects the text with the implied receiver, the Second Person, in the enunciation. In this way the text is also connected with the presupposed discursive reason, truth, or ideologically given consensus (common assumptions) in the logical space. The logical space connects the space of reality and the space of speech with the entire discourse of the text, that is, with the background texts that everywhere form the logical precondition and common sense for the individual text. Ultimately, it is discourse that constitutes the text's significative, meaningful connection with social reality as ideological and textual representation. The presentation in the text of (parts of) this social reality is the object of the analysis of discourse.

INSCRIPTION OF DISCOURSE

The speaking or writing individual is not heard only when an "I" appears in the text. The sender of the text appears much more frequently as an instance that administers and organizes the text's thematic and narrative subject matter with the help of the text's *quotations and anchorings* and by virtue of the various forms of speech acts and modalizations with which the text's Second Person is met when the subject matter is presented. In the case of schizophrenic patients, anchoring, quotation, speech act, and modality are decisively altered both in the creation of the text and in the ability to communicate. In the rest of this chapter and in the following chapters we shall try to show in what way the anchoring and quotations are altered and what effects the changes have on the speaking and thinking of the schizophrenic patient as well as on the listener. The place from which the speaking individual gets his or her linguistic expressions (i.e., *signifiers*) for the content (i.e., *the signified*) of his or her communication is not the same as the place or the spaces represented in enunciation. The place of the signifier has an independent influence on the speaker's presentation of the text. Classic psychoanalytic theories of the individual operate with the twofold concept of consciousness and the unconscious in connection with thought and language. When analyzing the patient, the psychoanalyst sees time and again that the patient's consciousness is not adequately equipped for self-understanding and insight into the psychic causes of his or her illness. Therefore, the psychoanalyst carries out a close reading of the *speech* of the patient and constructs or, to be more precise, reconstructs *another speech* behind or under the more or less direct, self-conscious speech. This other speech is both a part of and a product of the unconscious.

We should like to emphasize here and in the following material that the other speech (in or from the unconscious, as some psychoanalysts say) does not fundamentally differ from the speech that takes place in the conscious space of the enunciation, where one thinks that "one knows what one is saying." Rather, this other speech is characterized by being signifiers, where enunciation carries content. It is not possible to understand or realize what is being said in the other speech. Nevertheless, the speaking individual is always and everywhere obliged to organize his or her enunciation with the aid of the other speech. Thus, the other speech functions as a depot or storehouse for any communication. But how can this doubleness between the speech of the enunciation and the other speech be explained conceptually, and how is the other speech organized?

In accordance with the view of the text sketched in the first section of this chapter, we can characterize the other speech as *discursive*. For the individual who produces a text of one kind or another, the other speech does not, however, function as a kind of complete discourse, that is, as a textual entity that is unambiguously organized in a cohesive structure. For the individual, discourse functions as *partially dependent unstable relations among signifiers*. As a counterpart of discourse—understood as a socially abstractly defined totality of texts in a certain order—we can define the area of operation of discourse in the individual user of language as a *discursive register*. The discursive register is individual insofar as it is partial, but it is mentally, linguistically, ideologically, and consciously accessible. It can be analyzed from the point of view of linguistic theories, theories of consciousness, and psychoanalytic theories of the individual (describing his or her ideology, language and practice as a whole, and the dependence of these on upbringing, social class, working conditions, education, and so on).

The origins, specific character and mode of functioning of the discursive register in the individual user of language is the object of detailed consideration in psychoanalysis. From the point of view presented here, psychoanalysis—and its manifold activities—consists of technical, practically applicable rules for a textual analysis that investigates the relation between the individual discursive register and social discourse. Psychoanalysis performs a special kind of textual analysis. Its object is not just the discursive register; it is, more properly, the special relations of this register to discourse. Psychoanalysis, furthermore, is able to classify the various forms of (socially determined) discourse. It provides distinctions among, for example, perverted, neurotic, and psychotic discourses, each of which characterizes the individual in relation to a generalized discourse. Freud's presentation of his interpreting work in connection with his patients' retelling of their dreams clearly illustrates the way in which psychoanalytic classification operates with whole masses of discourse that are related to the discursive register of the individual.[10] He not only links the single, special elements of the dream—or more precisely, the dream's textual expression—to the cultural context that the discourses constitute, he also constantly links the dream as a whole, its structure and logic, to these discourses. The dominant discursive context that Freud shared with his patients was by and large of a literary nature. It consisted of the classics of Western European fiction with an admixture of current anecdotal material and its individual adaptation into the patient's life history. Freud's choice of discursive relations was an expression of the common ideological context that he shared with the middle-class and lower-middle-class with whom he worked. And it is this fellowship of discourse, as Lacan points out, that is the field of psychoanalysis: the so-called *symbolic order.*

Discourse is the system through which the other speech fixes the individual to the socially subjective. Discourse exists individually as a register in speech and socially as a socially organized form of expression. At the beginning of this century, the Swiss linguist Ferdinand de Saussure described language as a system of signifiers and signifieds in a structure that is defined by the differences between the elements.[11] We can identify discourse in the same way, not as a system of language, but rather as a *system of text.* Discourse has been roughly described as a text system by the Marxist theory of consciousness and of ideology as well as by sociopsychological theories of personality. Also, in these theories it is through discourse that the individual becomes a social being and is thereby equipped with a relatively limited but at the same time relatively precisely localized identity.

Apart from some few exceptional situations, however, the individual's binding to discourse cannot be known. It is not possible for the individual simply to acquire any real knowledge of what relations exist between the discursive register and discourse. On the other hand, the binding can often be experienced in situations where one is thrown off balance. Freud's studies of everyday slips of the tongue, reading errors, jokes, and wordplay amply document the existence and function of this binding.

The binding arises by virtue of a systematic and structurally stable inscription of signifiers in a relatively ordered and logical form of text. The individual discursive register is where inscription takes place. It appears from the above that the unconscious is the most marked property and mode of operation of the discursive register. By this we do not mean that the discursive register has been fully described. That is not the case. Some of the other important functions and properties of the discursive register arise from the way in which the inscription of the discourse, for the most part, takes place.

Inscription takes place neither fortuitously nor arbitrarily. In the course of the individual's long development it takes place primarily as a constant dialectical process regulated by the immediate conversational relations the individual takes part in. These conversational relations take place during the development of the law that psychoanalysis calls *transference* and that Freud found useful in his analytical work.[12] "This fact of transference soon proves to be a factor of undreamt-of importance, on the one hand an instrument of irreplaceable value and on the other hand a source of serious dangers," he writes, and the doctor-patient transference is thus defined: "the patient sees in him [the analyst] the return, the reincarnation, of some important figure out of his childhood or past, and consequently transfers on to him feelings and relations which undoubtedly applied to this prototype." Greenson, the psychoanalyst, describes transference in the same way as "the experiencing of feelings, drives, attitudes, fantasies, and defences towards a person in the present which do not befit that person but are a repetition of reactions originating in regard to significant persons to early childhood, unconsciously displaced onto figures in the present."[13]

The inscription of textually organized signifiers in any individual takes place mainly under the influence of the important function of transference: the repetition of an early relationship often determined by the family. Any schoolteacher or kindergarten teacher knows these conditions for inscription (or learning, as many people would call it). Even such an innocent process as reading—books, articles, newspapers—of necessity requires a stable transference relation if one is by any means to learn something from reading.

The important point about the inscription of discourse comes from the fact that the individual has a special way of relating to the source from which textual expression stems—that is, as subject to the law of transference. In transference's repetition of this special way of relating, from the individual's earliest years, there is incorporated *an instance in the individual that functions as the bearer of the inscription of discourse.* This instance has been described in many, frequently divergent ways. In psychoanalysis it would seem to be closely connected with the imprinted idea of the father and his exercise of authority as, for example, in Freud's descriptions, called the individual's superego. "The child's parents, and especially his father, were perceived as the obstacle to a realization of his Oedipus wishes; so his infantile ego fortified itself for the carrying out of the repression by erecting this same obstacle within itself. It borrowed strength to do this, so to speak, from the father, and this loan was an extraordinarily momentous act. The super-ego retains the character of the father, while the more powerful the Oedipus complex was and the more rapidly it succumbed to repression (*under the influence of authority, religious teaching, schooling and reading*), the stricter will be the domination of the super-ego over the ego later on—in the form of conscience or perhaps of an unconscious sense of guilt" (italics added).[14]

It is not our intention here to discuss any further the many different psychoanalytical theories about this instance. Instead, we shall attempt briefly to sketch the functions that this instance performs in the speaking individual, especially in relation to the discursive register. We can now say—taking as our point of departure the definition of transference as the law by which any inscription takes place—that the speaking individual must take a double position, partly as a *receiver* of textually organized signifiers in the discursive register, and partly as sender of speech in the enunciation. In the discursive register the individual relates to the instance of inscription in the ways laid down by the transference relations, that is, as *subject* in the true meaning of the word. The subject must submit to this instance in the same way as the small child must submit to the omniscient authority of the father or the pupil to the authority of the teacher. The subject—the individual as receiver in the discursive register—is therefore in principle ignorant. As Lacan says, it must be characterized as an "ineffable, stupid existence."[15] On the other side, the instance of inscription appears in principle to be omniscient, as a *subject-who-is-supposed-to-know*, to use Lacan's term. It is in the subject-who-is-supposed-to-know that the inscription of discourse takes place. It is here that we find the place of the signifiers in the speaking individual. The subject is addressed by, and gets answers to, his or her questions and receives every expression for his or her state from this subject-who-is-supposed-to-know.

Vis-à-vis the subject-who-is-supposed-to-know, the subject—and thereby the individual as such—can act only retroactively (or *nachträglich*, as Freud terms it). This is because the subject-who-is-supposed-to-know always appears in the *form of repetition in the transference relation* and because language that is articulated in the subject-who-is-supposed-to-know is *always already there before the individual's speech*. In contrast to the *other* whom the individual speaks to in the concrete situation, we can now identify this subject-who-is-supposed-to-know as a third party in any kind of speech and thought, that is, as the individual's *Other*, and we can schematically sum up these identifications (see Table 2.2).[16]

The existence of discourse in the speaking individual thus effects a *relation between the Other and the other*. This happens on the levels of discourse and enunciation, respectively, as the relationship to the other (who is actually being spoken to) is on the part of the individual doubled by the relations that control the individual on the level of the discursive register. When we relate

Table 2.2. The simple discourse-enunciation model

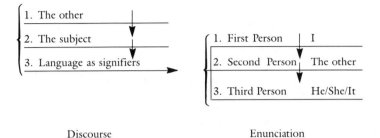

Discourse   Enunciation

to the world around us as acting, talking, and thinking individuals, we do it likewise via the Other. As an instance imprinted in the discursive register, the Other provides the means by which we establish our relation to our surroundings and to the objects, activities, and persons there. Psychiatric descriptions of schizophrenic patients' way of relating to their surroundings are built on the fact that this relationship has been altered to a degree that makes it difficult or impossible to achieve meaningful and emotionally stable contact with them.

CHAPTER THREE
DEIXIS AND THE REPRESENTATION OF REALITY

DEIXIS IN SCHIZOPHRENIA

I. Do you always refer to yourself as "we"?

P. Yes, because we are many people. Then, you see, I can . . . actually I don't always say it, but I know they hear and are listening to it, and then it's all right for me to say . . .

I. Hm.

P. Yes. When we are many people.

I. Have you ever told the police?

P. Yes, we have, um, in Øster Søgade [a street in Copenhagen], we talked to the police there when it was difficult, we couldn't cope. And that helped us, then, they have been there a couple of times. Yes.

I. How many times have they been there?

P. I can hardly remember, for there also used to be a Miss A . . . A. P. there, and there were difficulties with that lady, too. That lady preferred to beat them down all the time.

I. Hm.

P. And then . . . and then there was . . . we had to tell the police because that lady was a terrible nuisance. Yes. How many times I don't remember.

I. Hm.

P. But you can talk to the police about that. It's Øst . . . it's Øst . . . it's Østerbro [an area of Copenhagen] police station.

I. Østerbro police station?

P. Yes.

I. Um, at home, do you sit and think about these things, or what do you do at home?

P. Well, now they've got *Berlingske Tidende* [a well-known Danish newspaper], so I read *Berlingske Tidende* aloud. There are twenty from different planets who listen to it, and one from this planet who listens to it, and if there is anything which must . . . can be helped through the newspapers, I can't see what it is, but they know what it is, and if there is anything there machines or children or anything which should be helped . . .

I. Who can see it?

P. It, they those who listen from different planets, there are twenty thieves [Danish *tyve* can mean either "twenty" or "thieves"] or maybe more who listen from different planets, perhaps there are some from different, what shall I say, departments or trisks and svilts [patient's neologisms] and to people, and there is also someone from this planet who listens, yes. And so I read the newspaper aloud when I get the opportunity. Or, read aloud or show them the pages and they have to look for themselves because I can't see . . .

I. Can you talk to these trisks and svilts?

P. Well, they don't speak to anyone. But a wire can be attached to them, then they're able to speak. [In Danish the pronouns for "you," *De,* and for "they," *de,* are phonetically identical.]

I. Hm. Have you attached . . . ?

P. No, I don't speak with them. We're not allowed to speak very much. A tape explains it to us.

I. Hm. That means that you don't think you are speaking yourself? It's a tape that's speaking?

P. Yes, it's a tape that's speaking.

I. Hm.

P. There isn't anything that . . . it's not people speaking. It's a tape that's like in the Parliament, there they also have, I don't know who, they have tapes there too. They talk . . .

I. They have tapes in the Parliament?

P. Yes, there . . . they have tapes they talk on. But it's the same, you know, trisks and svilts, you know, it's the same, when one has tapes, it's the same.

I. Oh . . .

P. Yes, they don't really care when one has tapes. They don't pay any attention to that.

This is an interview conducted with a calm and well-spoken seventy-year-old female patient.[1] She showed no sign of dementia and was not undergoing psychopharmacological treatment. In the sequence of the interview reproduced here, it is not very difficult to find a number of characteristic phenomena within the registers of discourse and enunciation. Let us take as our starting point the descriptions offered by the patient herself of her recorded speech, in order to map some of the characteristic structures built around the First Person in schizophrenic speech. The nature of these structures is demonstrated in various ways by the interview quoted here. Most of the interviewer's questions aim to identify the deictic phenomena relating to the First Person, which are obviously of considerable importance for the patient's perception of herself and her surroundings. The interviewer approaches these problems both directly and indirectly, and it is worth noting that the patient replies to the questions in a fairly uniform way regardless of the interviewer's approach. The patient's presentation is thus relatively stable, indeed, in several respects chronic. In the First-Person position in the patient's enunciation we see at least three primary pronominal forms, the elements "I," "we," and "they." The patient's difficulties in expressing her personal view, including her view of herself, are caused in the first place by certain phenomena in her enunciation: it seems that the element "I" is replaceable by several other elements but that at certain, apparently unguarded moments it is present as an explicit pronoun covering the unstable First Person in the enunciation. One of the reasons that the First Person is both unstable and replaceable is that its "I" is characterized by not knowing and not being able to do what is normally required of a speaking "I":

. . . *I can hardly remember,* for there also used to be a Miss A. . . . A. P.

. . . *I can't see* what it is, but they know what it is

. . . perhaps there are some from different, *what shall I say,* departments or trisks and svilts . . .

Or, read aloud or show them the pages, and they have to look for themselves, *for I can't see* . . .

No, *I don't speak with them.*

Unlike the singular form "I," the element "we" causes a split in the enunciative fixed point of normal speech; and in this case it is obvious that it refers neither to the I / You-relation in the enunciation of the conversation (the interviewer and the interviewee in conjunction) nor to some group of people (an association, a family, a party, or the like) outside the interview situation. Instead, the speech projects a sort of multiple sender, multiplied by virtue of its very replaceability ("I," "they," "one" who has tapes). The last element frequently appearing in the First-Person position is "they." It refers to a series of elements in the patient's *fable* (structured narrative of a stable nature). We shall return to these elements in subsequent chapters, but we may mention their existence here. Most of them concern patients' representations of the relation of body to surroundings: they are elements of the type "people" who have "got stuck" or "have slid out" of the body shell, out of "the skin" that the patient perceives her body to be.

It is notable that the formal contact between interviewer and patient remains intact. The patient acknowledges that this is an interview and willingly replies to all questions. But some of the replies demonstrate that the boundaries between the space of reality, the space of speech, and the logical space are plastic and flexible. Questions directly pertaining to the patient here and now are often answered with reference to outer space (e.g., "planets"): local and global elements merge, as mentioned in Chapter 2. And even the space of speech with its person-related types of deixis appears unstable. We cannot assume that there is in the interview a common perception or identification of time, place, and parties to the conversation. The patient replies to questions concerning the First Person in a strangely indirect way:

I. Can you talk to these trisks and svilts?
P. Well, they ["they," not "I"] don't speak to anyone. But a wire can be attached to them, then they're able to speak.
I. Hm. Have you attached . . .
P. People have been put into them, then they can speak.

The Second-Person pronoun "you" has been carried over into

the reply as the Third-Person pronoun "they." Note that the interviewer repeats the personal pronoun to guard against any misunderstanding of the meaning; note also that it is only after three remarks have been exchanged that the patient even begins to reply to the question as a question about the fixed point of her own speech (i.e., as a question about the First Person of the enunciation). And then the reply is *in the negative:*

I.   Hm.
P.   No, *I don't speak* with them. *We're not allowed to speak* very much. *A tape explains* it to us.

This is a remarkable sequence "I," "we," "a tape" and it ends, appropriately enough, with the statement "It is a tape that's speaking." In Chapter 2 it was established as a general proposition that speech is organized in different dimensions corresponding to the degree or strength of the reference functions (types and forms of deixis). In the narrowly defined space of reality, the speaker is connected with the text by his bodily presence; in the case of the patient in this interview, this connection between body and speech seems to be lacking. When faced with direct questions, the patient replied as follows:

I.   Yes. But does anyone know *your* name?
P.   N-no, it's the same thing. They say we, um, they call us N. N. or something like that.
I.   N. N.?
P.   N. N.
I.   N. N.?
P.   Yes, N. N.
I.   Who called you that?
P.   Well, that's what they called us in the parish, I think they said that was our name.
I.   But it wasn't your name?
P.   N-no, I don't know. I don't know rea—— because it doesn't exist, that skin, it is, there are no people in it. It's a tape that's speaking. There are no people in it, the skin.

The elementary connection of body with speech in the space of reality does not work for this patient. More explicitly: there is no connection between the body and the First-Person pronouns in the enunciation and their "official," socially valid, lexical designation: the proper name. The interviewer therefore pursues his questioning:

I.   Don't you yourself feel alive?
P.   Well, ye-es, they . . . vicar's wives are alive.
I.   But you?
P.   It's the skin.
I.   . . . as a person are alive?
P.   N-no, I don't know what that is. It can, it doesn't exist, of course, there are no people in it. They have slid out. There was a gentleman in there, and that gentleman slid out, I believe it was yesterday or the day before. We didn't know that. And then these blocks slid out, they slid out yesterday, and I let them slide over into the sugar pools to make them come alive.
I.   Was it a gentleman?
P.   N-no, it . . .
I.   . . . and some blocks inside *your* skin?
P.   . . . was a gentleman in there, in the skin we didn't know that, and that skin then, that gentleman then became incorporeal and slid out, was, found a home and slid out.
I.   But was it out of *your* skin.
P.   Yes, out of it, the tiresome skin.
I.   Out of the skin you are wearing now?
P.   The tiresome skin, it . . . yes, you can see.
I.   Did it help you that that gentleman slid out?
P.   No, I had no idea that that gentleman had slid out, it, "Well, um, now I will slide out, I, I can manage now, I, I am incorporeal, so I may as well slide out." But then all of a sudden six hundred blocks slid out. They called them, they said it was six hundred blocks. It was, I don't know, they were both trisks and svilts and people, and then we let them slide out into the sugar pools for there they come, there they are dissolved and can come . . . can manage better until they can have a home.
I.   Then you feel that you (they) ["they" or "you"] are dissolved?

At this point in the interview we may note how difficult it is for the interviewer to ask any questions at all that can be answered unambiguously as questions about the patient's person. What is being talked about? Sugar blocks or persons?

I.   Then you feel that you (they) are dissolved?

P.   N-no, they are dissolved, what's it called, slide apart, I suppose, the block slides apart.

I.   Yes. What about you, are *you* dissolved, too?

P.   No, that skin? Well, it turns t—— to nothing, I don't know what that is. We don't know what it is. It has no, there's no mind or anything.

I.   How do you feel youself inside the skin?

P.   Well, we've been very unhappy about where we were, because we couldn't cope with our task. It's a government task, of couse. We can't cope with it in such a place. We need to be by ourselves, you see. Yes.

I.   Did you have the task assigned to you by the government?

P.   N-no, that, it, um, you can take it, we know nothing about it [here the patient is referring to a piece of paper earlier shown to her by the interviewer]. No, let me show you . . . those ladies, they were, they have been in bed, so they haven't got stuck. And there are many. They were taken to a large building. There were many, there were people spying ev—— standing everywhere. And then they say, "Do you have the gas ready?" they said, so the ladies say, "Do you have the gas ready?" and then a little later they said, "Then we've got them when they are dead, then we've got them for three hundred things, then we'll put them, these in, all those who are here, then we'll put them into three hundred things."

I.   It sounds as if you, you feel you're being annihilated?

P.   This skin here?

I.   You! ["they" or "you"].

P.   The ladies?

I.   You!

P.   No. I don't know who "you" ["they"] are, I don't know, for there's no one, all people have slid out here. Yes.

As we said before, it is not in its formal aspects that this conversation seems to have been altered. It is rather the patient's representation of herself, of her own person, her "I", that is peculiar. The two participants in the conversation exchange remarks about particular topics, and this does not seem to cause any difficulties. ("How do you feel youself inside the skin?" "Well, we've been very unhappy about . . ." "But is it out of *your* skin?" "Yes, out of it, the tiresome skin"). What works less satisfactorily is the mutual identification of the topics, persons, objects, time, and space of the conversation. Formally, the patient replies to the questions asked; but actually, in terms of content, the interviewer's questions can hardly be said to have been answered. The entire anchoring system of the conversation is ambiguous and unstable; the enunciative elements of the text do not work in a normal and customary way. The phenomenon that we see displayed in the speech of this schizophrenic patient is one we shall be returning to again and again. The production of text in schizophrenia is characterized by *failure of deixis*. And since the deictic functions of the text are decisive for the speaker's representation of reality, we can now conclude that *the negative representation of reality in schizophrenia is characterized by failure of deixis.*

What is meant by a "negative representation of reality"? First and foremost, the schizophrenic patient's representation of reality is not subject to the control of the First Person in the enunciation (its "I," corresponding to Freud's definition of a *Real-Ich,* whose task it is to uphold the distinction between "internal and external by means of a sound objective criterion").[2] That the schizophrenic patient's representation of reality is negative does not mean that the patient has a negative, recalcitrant attitude or 'takes a gloomy view of things'. It means that the schizophrenic patient can no longer *render positive* the representation of reality in his or her speech. It is characteristic of a positive representation of reality that on one level it maintains the distinction between the registers of enunciation and of discourse and that on another level it sustains the instances of the enunciation. A negative representation of reality is characterized by a breakdown of the distinction between the registers and a concurrent failure of the basic I / You / Here / Now system of the enunciation. In the negative representation of reality, the discursive other speech appears on the level of enunciation in an unprocessed, unquoted form. This is often done by filling the several instances of the enunciation (First, Second, and Third Persons) as we saw in the interview above.

THE BREAKDOWN OF THE DISTINCTION BETWEEN THE INTERNAL AND THE EXTERNAL WORLD

In psychoanalysis, psychosis is defined precisely according to this criterion. Freud talks about "negative reality testing" (*Realitätsprüfung*), which characterizes schizophrenic persons.[3] In Freud's view, the schizophrenic person can no longer distinguish between the objects of reality and the objects of the fantasy, that is, distinguished between what is *perceived* in reality and *hallucinated* in fantasy. The individual's inner world (*Innenwelt*) and outer world (*Umwelt*) merge in schizophrenics, which allows the things belonging to the inner world, what is fantasized or hallucinated, to appear in the world of reality as if it were real, as if they were reality. Freud remarks that it is a fact that renders the treatment of schizophrenics difficult. The distinction between external and internal does not work properly. And this impedes analysis. Freud writes: "As is well known, the analytic situation consists in allying ourselves with the ego of the person under treatment, in order to subdue portions of his *id* which are uncontrolled—that is to say to include them in the synthesis of his ego."[4] However, this process immediately raises difficulties for the treatment of schizophrenic persons. "The fact that a co-operation of this kind habitually fails in the case of psychotics affords us a first solid footing for our judgement. The ego, if we are to be able to make such a pact with it, must be a normal one," that is, a nonpsychotic "I" with a positive orientation toward reality. "But a normal ego of this sort is, like normality in general, an ideal fiction," states Freud. So the distinction between schizophrenic and normal reality testing is not quite as simple as we might be led to believe at first sight.

The psychoanalytical concept of *reality testing* is rather ambiguous, and serious objections have been raised against its theoretical status, not least as a means of distinguishing between psychotic and nonpsychotic states. The chief objection to reality testing is probably that it rests on some dubious assumptions, one being that it rests on something that is concrete, perceptible by the senses, and common to all people. So when we have replaced the concept of reality testing with the concept of representation of reality, it is because reality always exists to the individual human being in a form processed or represented by discourse. Reality is social and not necessarily concrete, perceptible by the senses, and common to all people. In many societies it is, for example, neither psychotic nor out of touch with reality to be mumbling words of entreaty to a nonpresent being, deity, or the like. In other societies such behavior might easily be regarded as being far removed from reality or downright harmful. In other words, it is not a question of reality *as such* but rather of the discursive representation of reality. Different societies take different views of psychotic states. Thus, it is the representation of reality in the speech of a patient that is decisive for whether it is psychosis or not. (See Figure 3.1).

When the discursive other speech appears in the speaker's enunciation in an unprocessed form where quotations are not marked, the representation of reality becomes negative. To the

Figure 3.1. Letter from a now deceased schizophrenic patient. The church, army, housekeeping, and banking are all in one message.

Thursday, September 10th,——

Catholic Church in Maribo.

You are kindly requested to send
2 German Cruizers up here
they need Fat and Pork.

Your humble servant
[signature]
The National Bank.

Psalm No. 402

schizophrenic patient the experience is often one of voices which from the outside usurp the attention and take control of his entire life and welfare. The First Person is thereby weakened. The I becomes ignorant and incompetent, as we noted in the interview above. Outsiders (e.g., a "gentleman" "in the skin," "trisks and svilts and people") speak on the person's behalf as if the person had been turned into an automatically playing tape recorder. The alien speech is therefore often felt to be hostile and persecuting. In a letter to the chief psychiatrist one patient gave an admirably exact description of this development:

Letter to the Chief Doctor, Febr. 13th, 19——
Explanation on my having been *committed* to the *6th* Ward at *K.M.H.* and then to four different wards at *Skt. Hans Hospital;* and being considered unfit for a—life in freedom. —First, I have *in my home from the residents* of no. 11 as well as no. 13 f. inst. when playing the piano late in evening had to put up with the following: *namely that which has been called my* illness—that I have heard the most scandalous and merciless utterances not just about myself—but even about my long-deceased parents and entire family and at night when I had not sufficiently drawn the curtains there appeared on the walls and ceiling all sorts of images of pictures— belonging to historical personages—at other times I woke under the impression that I had been giving a lecture before legal and police authorities—as well as before other persons of high standing—but forced myself to regard it as foolish dreams—and soon this was entirely dispelled by again falling asleep—but then the whole thing took on a more and more aggressive character such as chatting in the "W.C."—water tap and when I was about to cook my dinner on the gas-ring—at first I took it as a rather naughty joke but as it expressed itself with increasing insistency I also expressed myself vehemently against *not* wanting to hear it—to this came then at night utterances of a somewhat coarse nature—almost unmentionable—like fuck your a, etc.—leave that aside—*in connection* with a sensation in my abdomen—as if something was about to pass out of me— so that altogether it gave me the impression of a very mysterious *indecent* attack upon me—during which I was prevented from carrying out my domestic duties and had to lie down in the daytime whenever it expressed itself—something I have never known before—as I have never had *any* sort of food disagree with me and never known the least upset inside me which is why from the whole way it expressed itself I had to speak of it as *inflicted upon* me—and if I was for instance reading a newspaper—it was to me like a repetition of my *thought* —on what I read—and if I was sitting with my needlework I felt when there was traffic from the street like a vibration in connection with a sensation in me—as mentioned above. Therefore as this

happened with increasing vehemence and frequency it reacted, I suppose understandably, in me unto the greatest resentment—the more so as I could not address myself to any *particular* person as guilty therefore— which is why I chose the only path open to me—namely loudly *inside* my flat—as all the while expressed itself *outside* my flat—and have thus *not* stepped into view of any person—or bothered any particular person,— this is then briefly what I was summoned to the police for—and from there committed to hospital as said before where as you know, the despair within me has expressed itself by incomprehension and ignorance about my position on the whole business, which I have been trying with the greatest might to reject—as something highly mysterious—foolish—in- deed, almost criminal to take part in,—but when I had then somewhat regained my composure—I thought, of course, to be spared suchlike in hospitals—but gradually *felt* and *heard* it express itself even there almost to a *higher degree*—and I had f. inst. an experience 1 night at K.M.H. as if the most horrible occurrences of a cruel nature were being perpetrated in the corridor adjoining the sick room—the next day I was asked by 1 doctor if I had something there—and last night as before—to which I indicated it as heard—at that he just nodded various utensils are used as a means of expression to frighten us with (as one learns by and by). This is how I feel—when somebody wants to ask me—how I feel?[5]

The expressions in the text that are in italics were underlined in the original letter by the patient. It is hard to distinguish what comes from the outside—"*ouside* my flat"—from what comes from the inside; the patient, for example, feels the necessity of drawing the curtains to avoid "all sorts of images of pictures." Next "the whole thing" takes on "a more and more aggressive character," forces its way into the patient's flat and occupies the W.C., the gas ring, and so on with a constant "chatting," which the patient eventually feels compelled to contradict: "but as it expressed itself with increasing insistency I also expressed myself vehemently against *not* wanting to hear it." In the end what comes from the outside is as if "*inflicted upon*" the patient, it becomes "like a repetition of my *thought*," as she reports. The breakdown of the distinction between external and internal gives the patient a deep "despair within me," which "has expressed itself by incomprehension and ignorance about my position on the whole business." The patient's representation of reality has become negative; the enunciation structure has collapsed; and the *other speech* has burst through. (See Figure 3.2).

Figure 3.2. Drawing with legend done by a schizophrenic patient. Note the strings or rays at the head and back. Apparently the patient feels controlled "from outside" at the same time as there is "chatting." The legend reads: "There is chatting on the left and preferably to bed 1 of Room F at the window today." The text below the line is probably not connected with the drawing. It reads: "printed so, and is this place" (a strong deictic indication).

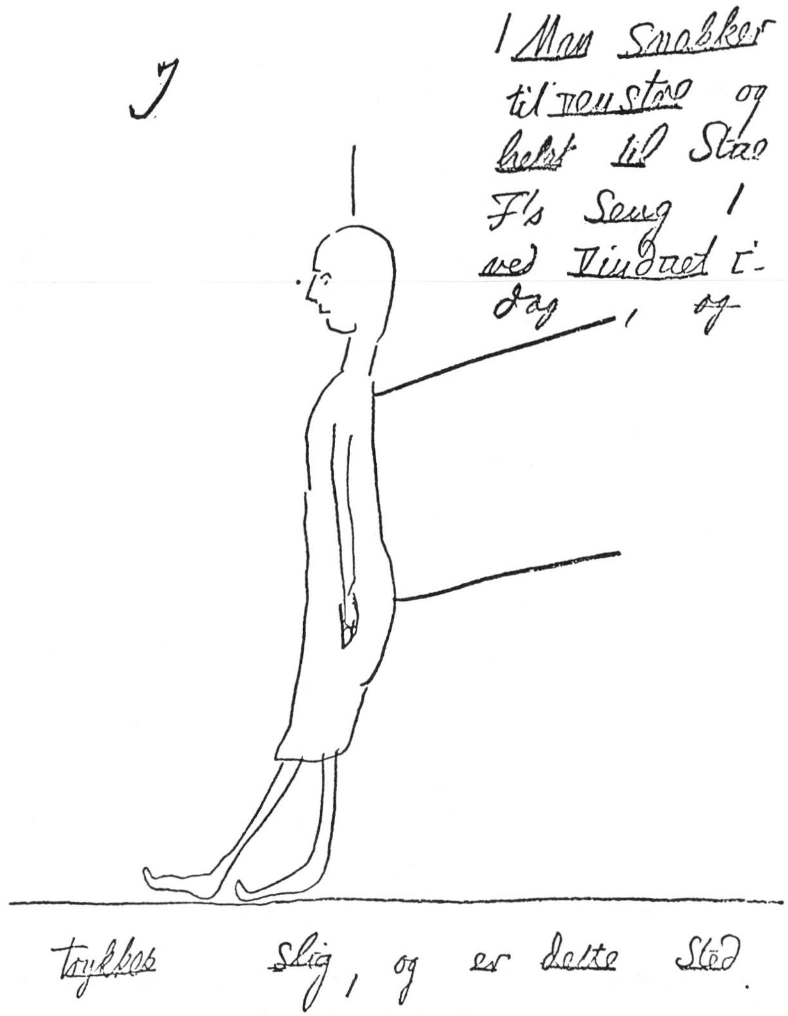

We will make no secret of the fact that what we have here defined as the basis for the way in which schizophrenia manifests itself is not *everything* that goes on. Already in the persecuted patient's letter to the chief psychiatrist we can see that there is some connection between the collapse of the stable instances of the speech and the speaker's perception of her body in relation to the different spaces, times, and persons in her surroundings. The numerous "utterances" occur "*in connection* with a sensation in my abdomen—as if something was about to pass out of me." Later the patient feels, when there is "traffic from the street like a vibration in connection with a sensation in me." We shall return to these phenomena in later chapters about the body (Chapters 5 and 6, about the imaginary body and about the body proper and the body of the other). For the moment, we shall limit ourselves to an account of the factors that are decisive for the form and content of schizophrenic speech. What do we mean when we say that the *other speech* breaks through in the enunciation of the schizophrenic patient?

ENUNCIATION AND THE DOMINANCE OF THE SIGNIFIERS

At the end of Chapter 2 we described how the production of text is everywhere subject to the conditions resulting from the relations between the register of discourse and the enunciation. On the one hand, the speaking individual occupies a subordinate position as a receiver of signifiers from the Other in the register of discourse—a prerequisite of any use of language that is socially acceptable and intelligible. On the other hand, speech is determined by the person spoken to, that is, by the Second Person of the enunciation, the other, whether that person is actually present or merely exists "in the head" of the speaking, writing, or thinking individual. We noted that the duality of discourse/enunciation sets the conditions for the production of text and that in schizophrenic text this duality is constituted in a peculiar way. The boundaries between the different deictically determined spaces becomes labile, and both the *forms* and the *types* of deixis undergo functional changes. In this chapter we have seen how deixis of person is changed with respect to the First Person in the enunciation, and we may add also that the forms of deixis (symbolic, anaphoric, and gestural) are changed in schizophrenic speech. Especially anaphoric deixis—whose function is to maintain a stable structure of references within the text—seems more or less to cease functioning, so that references are made to elements that have not been mentioned before but that nevertheless are expected to be familiar, or to mutually contradictory times, places, persons, and circumstances, as we saw in the interview at the beginning of this chapter. With regard to gestural deixis we may briefly mention the often extraordinary lack of conformity between body expression and linguistic expression, observable in many schizophrenic patients. For our purposes, however, it seems reasonable to regard these phenomena as another manifestation of the fundamental changes of deixis characteristic of schizophrenic persons.

As will be seen in the following chapters, and as we have already suggested, there is a clear correlation between the speaker's *body,* that is, his imaginary body (not the body as biologically and physically defined) and the speaker's *language,* in particular its deictic mechanisms. Moreover, a number of studies have shown that it is not only schizophrenic adults who have difficulties in mastering deixis; psychotic children also show signs of unmistakable deictic failure. A study of the linguistic achievements of autistic children has clearly documented that—unlike both normal and mentally retarded children—autistic children show signs of having very serious language-learning difficulties, "especially," the study concludes, "in the areas surrounding deixis in language."[6] The various kinds of deictic failure in language is what we here describe as the breakdown of the boundaries between discourse and enunciation. When this occurs the times, places, persons, and circumstances of the enunciation become diffuse, unstable, and replaceable entities.

One patient gave this description in a letter to the doctor:

> That which flows along the path of my life discharged more strongly in the last "six" years. By this is only meant the outer pulling system (peeple perhaps Natzis) inner net's criminal system or at eny rate the system (pull a pull, to finger pull (alla France but only alla The France) flowing from there That is wat one supposes is French only with the difference that it possibly is pull aces of production, that which shoots (comes as a press shoot, 2 kins one until a vibration of the skin if felt) But there is also something that is called the slider (these operate like a gun) Through these day and night haluxinations can be transmitted which again are read as series of dreams or thoughts. This works like hypnosis blows or shots. The stronger vibration at the genitals is called coarser grains) (What was behind Rasputin's reputation criminal in Bavarria behind longshot against the Court (*if that were it*) result collapse (Possible release to (flight of murder robbery) during action (production) A system of burning victim. It should be noted here that the slider passes through almost unnoticed takes more (intelligent victims) These are hunted by a criminal (pull set) This can *burn* child and woman) . . . [7]

Later in the letter the patient tries to hold on to the elementary instances of the enunciation in the torrent of signifiers that are triggered with mechanical promptness by certain nucleus words (like, e.g., "pull" or "pull system," "production," and "criminal"), a flood of expressions that in the letter are described in so many words as "That which flows along the path of my life." However, the patient succeeds only to a very limited extent in holding on to the instances of the enunciation. Note how the fable takes over:

> This was a body which also contain these pull system Also had pull aces even during the war, Possibly mostly female at that time. And now I come to the things sensed, seen and heard by me Which stands or touches contact with my person. As I am not very good at orthography and composition this can perhaps be analyzed as being somewhat incoherent, *Against me and my person production's is to sublement the criminal's assault on the victims,* and divert the attention.) A possible chain of Male and Female robbery chain And can out of the things existing in society both transport itself and at the same time create for itself a gown cover however not a monk's gown, seductively coaxed and phrased it can provide cover's (and deposits of criminals of that calibre in their 100.000s, There comes now a little of what happened close to my person And which is a pulling releasing pull. There in a hypnosis pull it pulls aright at the same time restrain the victims in getting to Father Mother, and proper authorities' knowl-

edge. And be drawn by means of pressure = the hypnosis slider. . . .
[italics added]

The enunciation is clearly dominated by the schizophrenic fable,
which in this case is about the persecution of the patient by a
comprehensive network of criminals, among whom is a murderer
who "attacks across the country as well Also places his projectiles
the trigger on victim, There was near my situation in Aarhus shot
a charge so powerful that I said 80 per cent more than I was the
cause of to the medical officer, who was surrounded by a few
hundred people." On account of this persecution the patient thus
speaks "80 per cent more" than he actually wants himself. The
speech takes on independence while the First Person in the enunciation seems to disappear "behind" the words of the fable:

> This burner barrel possible comes all the way from the south (via an
> original skeleton of burner lines advanced in advance. This line operates
> like a production's with the hand down to the trigger This can be released
> quite shut from behind with release over my person away.

The other speech "abolishes" the speaking First Person ("with
release over my person away") and now has free scope: it is now
the others—whether they are criminals, people, tapes, or trisks
and svilts—who govern the expressions of the speech, not the
speaker himself. The speech is addressed to the Other often in the
guise of the chief psychiatrist or some grand and important per-
sonage; but at the same time the speech is controlled by the
Other: the message appears to be turned in upon itself, as both
the First and Second Persons of the enunciation have disintegrated, and the text as a whole been "mechanized." We can represent this formally as an embedded enunciation without quotation
marks (see Table 3.1).

When speech is thus taken over by alien elements that produce
utterances that are not by any means necessarily true but are often
perhaps rather the opposite of what the patient wants to say, the
schizophrenic patient may get an unpleasant feeling that his
words, his thoughts, and his speech as a whole are forcibly taking
on an independent and alien character of a special kind.

Table 3.1. Model of discourse and enunciation for schizophrenic texts

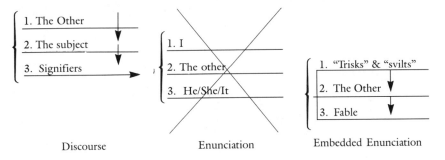

| Discourse | Enunciation | Embedded Enunciation |

In linguistics the usual stability of the relation between the signifier and the signified is related to the concept of *the sign*. In schizophrenic speech, this stability has given way to a situation where the signifiers are dominant. The content is no longer guaranteed by a Second Person present in the text. The different varieties of trisks and svilts who "can speak" "if a wire is attached," and so forth are not necessarily intelligible to the "I" that has changed functioning in enunciation. The signifiers of the Other are unrelated to the other in enunciation. Since these signifiers are not organized in accordance with the other in the enunciation, no stable sign relations are formed. Freud said about the language of schizophrenics that it was characterized by the same sort of logic as that obtaining in dreams. "The dreamwork, too, occasionally treats words like things, and so creates very similar 'schizophrenic' utterances or neologisms."[8] The sign is threatened—as well as threatening—in schizophrenia. The signifiers of the other speech dominate.

CHAPTER FOUR
AUTISM AND THE CONVERSATIONAL CONTRACT

TRANSITIVISM

In schizophrenic speech, the representation of the Other is hampered and at times impossible to discern. Classic psychiatry has registered this fact as a symptom or clinical picture: autism.[1] Autism is described as a process in which the conversation partner's connection with the text is gradually effaced or obliterated: the psychiatrist cannot find himself in the patient's speech. The listener (the psychiatrist) no longer understands the patient's speech, since the listener's understanding is being ignored by the speaker himself, by the First Person in the enunciation. In such cases psychiatrists will say that it is no longer possible to enter into the patient's feelings and that the patient, on his side, has lost his empathy with other people. It is a feature of schizophrenic speech—and the silence inherent in that speech—that, as the representation of the Second Person is being made increasingly difficult, an invisible third party steps between the partners in the conversation. As the conversation progresses, this third party, the Other, often virtually assumes control of the patient's speech. The Other interferes, interrupts, directs. Indeed, the Other structures the speech of the schizophrenic in such a way that often it is to the Other and no longer to the Second-Person receiver that the schizophrenic text is addressed (see the passage in Chapter 3 about the *dominance of the signifiers*). We shall deal more thoroughly with this matter in the present chapter.

As we established in Chapter 2, it is easy to observe how everyday conversation is conditioned by the Second Person. We see the effects of the other's presence, for example, in the illusions or unrealistic ideas of the neurotic, or in the hallucinations or delusions of the schizophrenic, but we also find them in the normal, socially well adjusted individual's more or less socially acceptable compulsive chatter, abstruse language, stammering and incoherent apologies, or plain silence. The effects of the other on the speech are seen in its theme (content), its logic (the way the content is fitted together to form units), in the syntax (sentence structure), and in the entire way the speech is presented (intonation, pauses, eloquent silences, etc.). But, although it is often quite obvious that the other has a strong influence on the speech, it can nevertheless be difficult to discern the regularities or the set pattern of this influence.

Schizophrenic speech reveals more clearly than any other form of speech the concrete influence that the other exerts on conversation. It is a familiar experience, when conversing with schizophrenic patients, as a partner in dialogue and not least as a therapist, that one enters into the enunciation as its Second Person only to be ousted again by the effective workings of the Other. Schizophrenic patients have this experience, too. Now and then, in their moments of *transitivism,* they complain that their thoughts are simply lifted out of their heads, or they complain that thoughts are imputed to them—sometimes by means of clever and obscure devices—that are completely alien, irrelevant, or outright hostile to them.[2] It may even get to the point where the schizophrenic person feels compelled, much against his own will, to keep giving expression to these alien thoughts in order to get rid of them. Usually, however, this transitivistic logic in the communication operates in a more covert way, so that somewhere in the speech it is stated that the schizophrenic patient's formulations have been "introduced" from the outside, that they are subject to "direction" or "remote control" from somewhere else, or things of that nature.

This somewhere else works as a symbolic organizer of speech.

The schizophrenic's speech is governed by the Other. The schizophrenic experiences the Other as a foreign body. It is an "influencing machine" operated from somewhere else, whose construction is inexplicable, incomprehensible, or invisible to the schizophrenic but that he must at all times seek to give expression to and describe.[3] We have argued above that the Other is a linguistically, psychologically, and actually existing symbolic phenomenon, an instance in the speech without which speech would not be possible. Here we propose to show, among other things, how the Other operates and governs schizophrenic speech in accordance with *transitivistic* processes.

The logic of transitivism is a general form of logic in schizophrenia. With a view to giving a description of this logic we will begin by reproducing part of an interview with a male patient:

I.   Why is this a good day to die?

P.   Because today I feel that I have achieved something which I have . . . I have thought for many years that I would like to exp—— to try to experience.

I.   And what is that?

P.   To be a media object.

I.   Has that been a great wish of yours?

P.   It has, actually, for a very long time, so that's why I'm completely cul—— curazy with delight; also because of the cigarette, however, I must admit.

I.   That's also "to be a media object," of course?

P.   Well, that depends on the way you look when you smoke; you see, if I sit shaking then it will have a deterrent effect. Because I, um, I am using the cigarette once too often and end up doing something like this, which I will never dare to do again. It simply hurt so terribly that I got my threshold of pain raised. Because that one is the first, that, those are some of the other . . . things up there, and I did this simply in a rage at a conference. [The patient indicates a line of scars from burns produced by lighted cigarettes.]

I.   Hm. Are you often in a rage?

P.   Um, I don't understand that. Are you being rude? I believe I am being used as light. Should we try to finish the recording here, because, well, we discussed that in the first recording, as well, when we were going to finish.

I. Well, that . . .

P. What will the cameraman say if we finish now? [The patient speaks via the microphone to the technician's booth, which he cannot see.]

I. He can't answer you.

P. Because I, I want to finish the second part there. And then we'll do a third, that is you know, the fourth dimension, don't you, and there are of course an infinite number of functions, and just as many visions, and then just as many dimensions, that's what I think. I can't do anything about that. Not for the moment. It's called to practice something.

I. What is it called?

P. It's called to practice something, some yoga like something, and, um, I know Dali, and I have only heard him, don't know him but, and Kundalini [In Danish *Kun-dalini*, literally translated, means "Only-dalini"] is a black cobra, which is to be taken to mean that, um, that the cobra black is a snake dark, but, um, it is also called Kundalini in those connections, I've read about it, yes, there really are books about it. I finished secondary school before I realized there was something called yoga.

I. Hm.

P. Simply. I grew up running. If you see what I mean. I am lame. You can hear it in this way. [The patient is *not* lame but gets up from his chair in the television studio and takes two steps forward and then two steps backward, stamping hard.]

I. Yes, all right.

P. And that would probably come through on the mike. Shall we finish our talk, then I'll smoke my last cigarette here, shouldn't I?

Let us concentrate first on some of the aspects of the dialogue relating to the stability and security of the conversational relationship. The stability—and with that, of course, the security—depends on what we have previously placed on the levels that determine the relationship between the Other and the other (see Table 2.2). What we placed there has to do with the transference relations of the conversation.

The concept of transference includes both the contract implicit in the conversational relationship and the enunciative stability on

which this contract depends. In the first three exchanges we see a
stable relationship between the partners in the dialogue. The
implied Second Person in the patient's enunciation is stable:
straightforward answers are given to the interviewer's questions;
the coherence and content as a whole could hardly be expected to
cause any difficulties in comprehension. In the fourth exchange
the interviewer's repetition of the phrase "to be a media object"
seems to have a certain effect on the media-conscious, almost
media-fixated patient. The interviewer's lame joke is taken literally and causes the patient to offer an explanation involving a
succession of topics: from the cigarette to the medium, from the
patient's "media image" (the patient is *not* a well-known person)
and on to his body. In a fit of rage the patient has branded his
own body, probably in protest against being "exploited" at the
conferences held in psychiatric institutions. This could be part of
the explanation for what suddenly occurs in connection with the
exchange where the interviewer asks:

I.   Hm. Are you often in a rage?

In response to this question the patient at first shows a marked
lack of comprehension:

P.   Um, I don't understand that.

With a stable Second-Person relationship in the enunciation—in
normal interviewing circumstances—the continuation would be,
for example, "Can I have that again?" or "Why should I be?"
However, here the answer is:

P.   . . . Are you being rude? I believe I am being used as light. . . .

In the remaining part of the dialogue, up to the concluding
exchange, the transference relations and thus the conversational
relationship are damaged in various ways. The position in the
enunciation that the Second Person ought to have occupied is
now invaded by a third instance, namely the TV cameraman

(representing the Other), who is absent from the studio but is present nevertheless because he is present in the technician's booth. The speech is now addressed to this absent and yet present instance, which cannot answer back and that in no way takes part in the interview. The sentence, "What will the cameraman say if we finish now?" is said neither to elicit an answer from the cameraman nor to convince the interviewer by means of some rhetorical trick. The interviewer's "He can't answer you" is ignored by the patient: the laws of verbal interchange have been set aside; the deictic anchoring in the space of speech fails; and the patient speaks on "into the air," carrying on what is, at least apparently, a monologue (without a Second Person *marked* in the enunciation). At the same time, the logic of the conversation is becoming more doubtful: "Should we try to finish the recording here, because, well, we discussed that in the first recording as well, when we were going to finish." Both the purpose and significance of the conversation as far as the patient is concerned are uncertain. The transference relations have been altered, and it is characteristic that on the one hand the patient wants to end the conversation ("because, well, we discussed that in the first recording as well," etc.) but on the other hand the patient does not, in fact, end it; it goes on until the relationship has been restored to a reasonable degree.

This concrete sequence of an interview shows in concentrated form some typical features of schizophrenic speech. It shows that in schizophrenic conversation periods with a high degree of enunciative stability (corresponding to the communicative contact, the conversational *contract*) alternate with periods having little or no contractual enunciative stability. In these latter periods we see a number of characteristic effects. The Second Person in the enunciation is shut out completely from the space of speech, while the First Person is masked or disappears. As a substitute for the actually present Second Person, a nonlocatable, nondeictic instance is introduced. In this interview it is filled by the remote cameraman.

To put it briefly, an exclusion of the Second Person in the

enunciation manifests itself in the speech as a failure of the entire deictic system: temporality, spatiality, and conversation partners are radically changed. We observe that the conversation is no longer carried on in a space that the conversation partners perceive as limited, one that can be defined in terms of time and space and where both parties have clear and well-defined social roles (see Fillmore's definition of deixis referred to in Chapter 2). Instead, the patient speaks *before,* or possibly *to,* a projective instance with Second-Person characteristics. In Chapter 6 we shall study this projective mechanism more closely. But the establishment of this new conversational space in the middle of an otherwise relatively normal conversation—provided it is possible to apply the term "a new conversational space" to these periods of flagging enunciation—is illustrated even more clearly by many of the letters written by schizophrenic patients. These letters are addressed, for instance, "To the Police of Berlin and Madrid, Berlin," "To Maribo Cathedral," "To Emperor," or "To the Chief Doctor," which recurs frequently. Whether the content of the letters is of any relevance to the addresses or not, the addresses seem to indicate that the Second-Person instance in the conversational space is now being upheld by names to which power, law, and order—preferably on some global or national scale—are attached:

> *To* the National and Local Police, Police Headquarters or and police station in Randers: city and county and district and etc.
>
> In the year 19——, in the month of October day 14 to da 21 (*both* inclusive or counted in), I, spending my holidays with the family in E., No. 73 V.-Street, 2nd Floor, I, name N. N. or N. N. Under hospital permission at the end 19——es. Denmark, occupation by the Germans, soldiers. State of emurgency, the state of emergency or the cessation of emurgency, *curfew,* the years 19——es, Danish, German, war: black-out times and times of rationing, authorities. Etc.

As will be seen, the new Second Person of the conversational space is a big name, and as in the interview with the young patient above, it is a frequently recurring characteristic that the content of the schizophrenic speech or letter shows how the letter writer tries to get a share in this new Second Person's authority. To write or speak to the Other is to *desire to be* (part of) the Other. (See Figure 4.1).

In Chapter 6 we shall show how this phenomenon is connected with the decay of the boundaries of the body—that is, with the permanently threatened boundaries of the distinction between outer and inner of the imaginary body. For the moment we may note that the conversational space of speech lacks delimitation and that this lack of delimitation contributes to the introduction of a substitute for the person spoken to.

ENUNCIATION AND THE DOMINANCE OF METONYMY

This substitution often comes about through a process where it becomes impossible to locate a receiver of the speech who is actually present, and the speech is instead addressed to a Third Person who is out of reach. The Second Person actually spoken to is replaced by ideological and institutionalized representatives of power, especially linguistic power, since it is, of course, those having linguistic power who give orders, decide, pass laws, and so on. (In Chapter 7 we shall return to the criticism of power

Figure 4.1. The introduction to a diary of about 200 pages written by a now deceased patient. Ecclesiastical and secular authority are here on a grand scale.

In the name of christ: —

Journal of the Writings of the Holy Spirit:

   According to Royal Court and Constitutional Documents, which are hereby written by Hs. Msty. King H Chr. [patient's name], who is at present created in God's image, which is also used for reliefs on coins bothe here in Denmark as well as in Spain:—

King of the Wends and Goths, which means in Danish:—King of the converts [Wends and Danish omvendt, which means "convert," are phonetically similar] and the good:—as well as Duke of Schleswig: Holstein: the Ditmarshes: Oldenburg:—Lauenburg: Stormarn: which means the seven Danish prefects as well as the Danish and Spanish King and Crown Prince, and also the servants of the Holy Spirit, both on this side of the Egguator as well as on the other side of also the Egguator, with area of sea as well as land: —

implicit in many texts.) Those having linguistic power are in possession of the law. And these representatives of linguistic power are (as if they were real) actual conversation partners. In schizophrenia one can write and speak both to God and to any Tom, Dick, or Harry.

But it is important to note that there is a persistent attempt to maintain the order of speech. Doing this is, of course, difficult for many patients, since the structure of speech—in particular its basic enunciation structure—has more or less broken down. In the interview the patient invokes the conversational or linguistic order in various ways. "I can't do anything about that. Not for the moment. It's *called* to practice something"; and later, "*which is to be taken to mean* that, um, the cobra black is a snake dark, but, um, it is also *called* Kundalini in those connections, *I've read about it, yes, there really are books about it.*"

We have said that the introduction of a substitute for the Second Person in the enunciation and the breakdown of the transference relations come about through changes in the deictic system of the speech. Concurrently, we can observe yet another change in the text, this time at the Third-Person level of the enunciation, at the level of what is being talked *about*:

P. Because I, I want to finish the second part there. And then we'll do a third, a third, that is, you know the fourth dimension, don't you, and there are of course an infinite number of functions, and just as many visions, and then just as many dimensions . . .

The speech becomes *metonymically substitutive*. This means that words and sentences are substituted for one another and follow after one another as a result of phonetic and semantic similarities and contiguities. The Second-Person instance in the enunciation is invalidated as these metonymies come to dominate the text. Finally, the Second Person in the enunciation ceases to guarantee the text's viewpoint, coherence, and logic. The question of *what* themes replace the otherwise established subject matter of the speech is one we shall return to; it is reasonable to suppose that there is more to the determination of metonymies than linguistic similarities and contiguities. But for the moment we want to emphasize that speech (text, communication) of a type that we would characterize as being metonymically substitutive and unstable in its enunciation can appear as schizophreniform speech.

In the interview—as in many other schizophrenic texts—metonymies abound; they are both semantic and syntactical in nature; and they play on a number of linguistic paradigms (such as numerical order, morphological endings, and so on). Moreover they are, in a very direct manner, connected with the ways the unconscious functions in that they consist of a number of phenomena of linguistic similarity and contiguity in which it is possible to recognize displacement and condensation. In the concluding remarks of the interview sequence we can see what goes on quite concretely: the metonymies occupy the phonological, semantic, syntactical, and entire enunciative organization of the speech: "in the first recording" leads directly to "the second part," which is supplanted by "a third, a third, that is"; and this is pursued further in "the fourth dimension," "functions," "visions," and so on. Finally, there is a cluster of expressions around terms like "Dali," "Kundalini," "cobra," "yoga," and so on where both form and content play a part. This accumulation (or overdetermination)[4] of signifiers will not be analyzed further in this context.

It is characteristic of nonpsychotic speech that previous enunciative relationships have a number of stabilizing effects on the enunciation of any particular speech. Together these effects provide the speech with a form that in itself is perceived as an expression of the speaker's character structure or personality. But whenever these previous enunciative relationships break through—as sudden recollections, oversights, slips of the tongue, or other symptoms for example—they will always be shown up by the speaker for what they are, textually speaking, namely quotations that belong in different contexts. That is to say, they will be represented—or excused—by the speaker by means of modality markings and clear deictic markings, which in various ways render the slip of the tongue, the recollection, and the like objective (see Chapter 2): "Oh, perhaps I said something there which . . ."; "Just imagine, yesterday I suddenly got the crazy idea that . . ."; or the complaint of the compulsive neurotic, "Don't you find it peculiar that the expression 'little black poodles' keeps popping up in my mind—I who hate black poodles!" In this way the First Person asks the Second Person that they, together, keep their distance from that which so unexpectedly and often unpleasantly crops up in his mind, and the effect is that the quotation preserves its character. The neurotic and the normal person are not, as a rule, thrown off course to any significant degree by quotations from previous enunciative relationships, although for the neurotic they *can* be quite compulsive and painful.

In schizophrenic speech, the picture is different. Here quotations break through, unmarked and unanchored: "It is also called Kundalini in those connections" (What connections?); or "That's what I think. I can't do anything about that. Not for the moment. It's called to practice something" (Who is supposed to have said that?). Let us consider yet another example. A patient once described how God pursued her sexually, or rather desired her genitals, which in passing were turned into God's own genitals. The interviewer asked "God said that to you?" to which the patient answered:

P. Yes, yes, and I wrote his discharge for Nazareth in Austria yesterday with my pencil.

This compact, complex, and overdetermined utterance appears to have been formed out of the remains of several different utterances stemming from other enunciative relationships than the present one. By and large, the utterance lacks anchorage. It seems to presuppose the presence in the enunciation, not of just one, but probably of many different Second Persons. When taken as a whole, these quotations in their fragmented form must be thought to provide those persons with a sufficient basis for the patient to be able to establish a space of speech. In reality, there is no space of speech that is common to both the interviewer and the patient. But let us consider the elements in the utterance separately:

discharge refers to the patient's frequently expressed wish to be discharged. One reason why the patient uses the expression "I wrote *his* discharge" instead of "*He* wrote *my* . . ." may be that, after all, the sentence is about God, who by definition possesses global power, and thus also the power to give the patient the freedom she desires so strongly. The patient's reversal implements *linguistically* what she would like to see implemented *in reality*. A second reason for the reversal could be that the patient simply identifies herself with God (the idea that her genitals are God's);

for Nazareth touches directly on the fable of God, the Almighty, the Liberator (from hospital), the Redeemer (sexually). There is a straightforward *metonymical sliding* from "God" to "Nazareth";

in Austria is probably the result of a *metonymical sliding* from town to country ("Nazareth" to "Austria"). Moreover, the patient lived in Austria for a number of years and actually later in the interview speaks German, a language she otherwise never uses;

with my pencil refers to a pencil accidentally lying in front of the patient during the interview. It is characteristic that this is another reversal, since the pencil belonged to the interviewer. Owning a pencil—like being God—becomes synonymous with possessing power, namely the power to effect discharges.

As will be seen, the task of decoding the enunciative relationships embedded in just a single sentence can be an exceedingly difficult one. The reason is that the utterances from which the different quotations originate presuppose several *different* Second-Person enunciative instances, which are here embedded in the *same* utterance. The Second Person varies from one phrase to the next. The implicit assumptions change. Therefore, the First Person of the enunciation is also not the same throughout. It is not the same voice we hear speaking. The *I* of the speech has almost disappeared.

THEMATIZATIONS OF THE OTHER

Normally, speech gives rise to contracts between the speakers. This happens by virtue of the text's semantic, enunciative, and discursive consistency. In schizophrenic speech, on the other hand, we see that the consistency has been replaced by the dominance of the metonymies and the consequent difficulties as a partner in dialogue with a schizophrenic (e.g., as therapist or as interviewer) in taking part in the establishment of contractual conversational relationships. Normally the First Person of the enunciation sees to it that the other "is in on" the semantic structure of the speech and, in this way, sees to it that an enunciation structure is built up that is either stable and centered around the "I" or, conversely, is clearly and consistently depersonalized or general. In contrast, the enunciation of schizophrenia is without a stabilizing Second Person, without clear quotational relations between the elements of the text, and thus without semantic coherence. The text is decentered. Its anchorage has slipped. The Other speaks through the enunciation. A patient gives this account of his experience of the *transitivistic* mechanisms: "Unfortunately, of course, everybody knows what I am doing. The thought-speech criminals send it out to my family."

In transitivism the Other speaks. It is, therefore, often to the Other one is speaking when, as a therapist or relative, one is speaking to a schizophrenic person. However, the Other is never an accidental or meaningless speech behind the speech of the enunciation. The Other is an ideologically implanted, linguistically existing fact in *any* socialized individual.

It is true that, with the schizophrenic patient, the shape of the Other seems to be the result of particular disastrous events. This does not alter the fact that we all possess an Other that always contributes to our ability to function in social and human relationships, to maintain the complicated enunciation structure that sustains our reason and judgment, and to distinguish between that which is outside ourselves and that which is inside ourselves (in the form of thoughts, ideas, fantasies, etc.).

In this context we shall not go into the various theories to be found within different psychiatric and psychoanalytic schools or trends. But we shall briefly repeat that the Other is an actively working supplier of signifiers from the register of discourse and that in schizophrenia the signifiers are organized metonymically in the enunciation. In schizophrenia the supply of signifiers by the Other takes place in a specific way: it is *experienced* by the schizophrenic. In his speech the schizophrenic talks about it: *the Other is thematized in schizophrenic texts.* This happens in ways that may seem unfamiliar, uncontrollable, and often unpleasant to the schizophrenic; see, for instance, the letter to the Chief Doctor (Chapter 3).

This supply of signifiers is only one side of transitivistic logic, only one side of the fact that, in the experience of the schizophrenic, *others* are in control of or *are* the real basis of speech. The other side has to do with the *Ersatzbildung,* the substitutive formation, which the organization of the signifiers constitutes at the level of enunciation. In schizophrenia, generally speaking, the presence of the Other at the level of enunciation causes special kinds of symptoms in the speech, among them metonymic substitution.[5] What is specific for schizophrenia is the experience of *reality* in the metonymic substitutions of speech, or generally: the experience of the Other as a phenomenon that is external, alien, and often very hostile. In the following chapter we shall give a more detailed description of the way the Other is organized in accordance with the speaker's *imaginary body.* And in Chapter 6 we shall show that the imaginary body is organized *doubly,* so that certain parts of the imaginary body are connected with the Second Person of the enunciation, whereas other parts are connected with the speaker's desire (in the form of the wish to become one with the person spoken to or to be in total accord with the partner in the conversation). Also in Chapter 6 we shall return to the present chapter's finding that the decisive feature of schizophrenia as a mental disorder is its special structuring of the Other as an effectively working instance that is present in the processes that produce speech.

CHAPTER FIVE
THE IMAGINARY BODY

THE FRAGMENTATION OF THE IMAGINARY BODY

This chapter deals first and foremost with the concept of *the imaginary body*. When discussing the phenomena of the imaginary body, psychoanalytical literature uses terms like "body ego," "self-representation" and "object representation," and "object relations." It is not our task here to order the many and often contradictory ways in which the concepts of body and representation are used. However, the concept of the imaginary body should neither be confused with, nor directly tied to the anatomy of the body, nor to the so-called neuropsychological body schemata,[1] even though these concepts of the body should by no means be dismissed as uninteresting. Without doubt, physiological factors play a part in the creation of representations of body, subject, and environment. But we are concerned with describing the logic of the imaginary body, that is, with identifying the laws that organize the structures and processes of the imaginary body both in socialization and in dialogue.

The imaginary body must be understood as an entity of organizing principles for the fantasmatic elements that partly anchor the subject in an unconscious discourse and that partly constitute the conscious and self-reflecting ego and its linguistic usage as "I." Fantasmatic elements are those which appear on the scene of fantasy. As well as being structured in advance, they have a structuring function.

The fantasmatic elements, or fantasms, are *signifiers*. They are structured insofar as their existence and presence in fantasy are determined by something else, namely a great number of different, individually varied, cultural, ideological, and historicobiographical circumstances in socialization. They are structuring insofar as they take an active part in the creation of the emotions and affect, in general, the linguistically articulated chain of fantasy that constitutes thought.

The imaginary body provides the mental preconditions for the very psychodynamic functioning of the human being. Body fantasms function in every imaginative activity and in any production of linguistic meaning. But these general definitions are by no means sufficient to define the concept of the imaginary body. It is most unlikely that texts can be found that, to the same extent as schizophrenic texts, thematize and fabulate about the body's universe with its frequently sinister, grotesquely twisted, and macabre *tableau-vivants*. Therefore, it is necessary to let the texts speak for themselves in the discussion of the body as a theoretical concept.

A male patient once wrote the following letter:

23.5 ———

Dear Servants,
I cannot get any peace here in this institution because of nurse A's gentle care. Her mild eyes persecute me day and night. Can you not take me to a rough place? I would prefer to go the following way: twenty stabs in the stomach (big and small), clinical treatment from Dr. Brünnicke, (suicide (anticlinical), active service, being drilled through the back hole and up out through the front passage with a sword, then crucifixion to a tree, finally duel in Skagen [a small town in Denmark] followed by deep cuts made by a doctor's hand or a clinician, having my right leg sawn off high up as well as being thrown to the lions and being boiled alive. I am a little unsure about this way but naturally I am always at your service.
[signature]

It is probably not difficult to understand the patient's uncertainty about the "way" he has suggested. But beyond that the details of the letter probably evoke some confusion in many readers. We shall return to the text later, but here we can establish that the

body the patient is referring to in connection with his sugges-
tions for treatment is an unconnected, fragmented, and damaged
one. We assume that the special schizophrenic slidings of subject
and meaning (which we analyzed in the previous chapters) are
determined by the ways the fantasmatic elements are organized
and circulate in fantasy and in speech. We sum up the relations
between the fantasms in schizophrenia under the term "fragmented [morcelé] imaginary body."[2] Let us look a little more
closely at the fragmented body.

The interview (Chapter 3, p. 44) continued thus:

I. The organs you spoke about before which were hanging at,
    um, at Dosseringen . . . ? [Dosseringen is a well-known street
    in Copenhagen.]
P. Oh, on Dosseringen?
I. Yes?
P. Yes?
I. Um . . . were they some of *your* organs?
P. Organs, no, you know . . .
I. You were talking about liver and kidneys . . .
P. No, it isn't Dosseringen, it's Øster Søgade [a street in
    Copenhagen].
I. Oh, sorry, Øster Søgade.
P. Yes, no, liver, kidneys and lungs, they slide out crushed be-
    cause they have very big sexual organs. And so they slide out
    crushed on many, many people.
I. Are they *your* organs?
P. No, they are people's organs. We haven't come down there.
    We have guarded ourselves well and we couldn't become in-
    corporeal.

"Liver," "kidneys," "lungs," and "sexual organs" are metonymically joined, semantically contiguous elements in the patient's
fable. They are "lexicalized" signs but without these signs' usual
anchoring in a dictionary, lexicon, or in some other reference
work. The position of the organs and their remarkable functions
could hardly be confirmed by consulting anatomy or physiology
textbooks.

In spite of their lack of lexical anchorage, the organs have a structuring function in regard to the patient's understanding of herself and her surroundings. Structuring, partly because the conversation seems to break down as soon as the interviewer reveals that he is not quite sure about the geographical position of the organs, either in the patient's fantasmatic geography or on the map of Copenhagen. The interviewer's refusal to accept the fantasmatic geography of the organs provokes a break in the conversational contract: the patient's reaction is one of astonishment, distance, and miscognition at what she regards as the interviewer's mistaken idea about the position of the organs. She does not try—here or anywhere else in the interview—to put herself in the position of the mistaken interviewer so that the parties to the conversation together can find a common ground, some common preconditions and references that can function as the basis for reestablishing and maintaining meaningful communication (see the definition of the concept of discourse in Chapter 2). This corresponds precisely with what we pointed out about the way schizophrenia excludes the Second Person in the enunciation.

Much of the literature about psychoanalysis and psychotherapy deals with the connection between the therapist's understanding and acceptance of the fantasmatic geography that functions in the dialogue and in the transference on the one hand, and on the dialogical contract of the working alliance on the other. We shall return to this in Chapter 8. In this chapter we shall first and foremost deal with other functions of the imaginary body.

As is well known, schizophrenic texts are not the only texts where body fables and thematization of the body's organs can be found. Apart from cartoons, paintings, and drawings (e.g., Brueghel's and Bosch's paintings and the baroque universe of organs found in the surrealists), poetry and fiction frequently contain descriptions of the organs of the body and the way they are interrelated in fantasy. The body—with all its various organs—is first and foremost depicted as that place which, more clearly than anything else, "tells the truth" about the way the individual and his surroundings exist and relate to each other.[3] Body language is often more reliable than the deliberate reflections of the rationally thinking ego. In popular novels—and for that matter also in the utterances of daily life, in sexual relations, or in arguments—the parties involved have to "look one another straight in the eye" or "feel their heartbeats quicken" when the real truth must come out. In other contexts we read about how the body absorbs the complete attention of the person when the ego is not its normal self. In these cases the body takes on the role of the surroundings in communication. This is, for example, the case with the experiences of the hero in detective novels where the hero, after having been badly beaten up, thinks that he hears *a voice in the vicinity*. In Raymond Chandler's *Farewell, My Lovely*, it goes like this:

> "Four minutes," the voice said. "Five, possibly six. They must have moved quick and quiet. He didn't even let out a yell."
> I opened my eyes and looked fuzzily at a cold star. I was lying on my back. I felt sick.
> The voice said: "It could have been a little longer. Maybe even eight minutes altogether. They must have been in the brush, right where the car stopped. The guy scared easily. They must have thrown a small light in his face and he passed out—just from panic. The pansy."
> There was silence. I got up on one knee. Pains shot from the back of my head clear to my ankles.
> "Then one of them got into the car," the voice said, "and waited for you to come back. The others hid again. They must have figured he would be afraid to come alone. Or something in his voice made them suspicious, when they talked to him on the phone."

On closer inspection—as the unfortunate hero gradually comes to—it appears that the voice is coming from the hero's own body or from parts of the body that have taken over the function of speech for a short time, by means of a hallucinatory reappearance in the external world:

> I balanced myself woozily on the flat of my hands, listening.
> "Yeah, that was about how it was," the voice said.
> It was my voice. I was talking to myself, coming out of it. I was trying to figure the thing out subconsciously.
> "Shut up, you dimwit," I said, and stopped talking to myself.
> (Raymond Chandler, *Farewell, My Lovely*.
> Harmondsworth, 1949: Penguin.)

This split between the "I" and the body, and the resulting possibility for projections—where the organs of the body make their return in the space of speech as speaking, demanding, and acting organs—raise the question of to what extent the function of the limbs and organs that dominate schizophrenic speech can be compared with the function of the depiction of the organs in fictional texts and poetic metaphors. What specific properties can we assign to schizophrenic body thematizations?

This question has a long tradition: psychiatry, psychoanalysis, and literary criticism have formulated the question about the relation of linguistic distortions in literary texts to the schizophrenic's pathological treatment of language. Here we shall limit ourselves to mentioning two points that are decisive in the treatment of schizophrenia: the establishment of the conversational contract and the formation of the imaginary body as a nonfragmented totality.

In literature the problematic thematizations of the organs occur in those cases where the speaker's "I" is no longer "backed up" by a self-image, that is, an image of the speaker's own body. When this "backing up" fails, the "I" loses its body-bound identity. It is in such crises of identity that body and organ thematizations can appear on the scene of consciousness as the speaking counterpart of the "I".

However, fiction insists on the contractual nature of the enunciation not being interfered with in that it is left to the built-in experienced reader—the implied Second-Person addressee—to put two and two together. Of course, concrete contracts can be at risk in such crises and sometimes things go too far, but this happens only so that the contracts can be reestablished or so that new and better contracts can be established between the persons in the text or between narrator and reader. In other words, the enunciation relations are preserved intact; even when the First Person loses his or her linguistically "correct" voice, the Second Person in the enunciation retains his or her position. This is, of course, radically different from what we pointed out in the case of schizophrenia. That the nonschizophrenic organ thematiza-

tions of fictional texts are "contract preserving" with regard to
both theme and narrative is reflected in the fact that in these texts
the body usually preserves a total form, that is, preserves its identity in a relatively stable linguistic structure. And lyrical or epic
texts, as a matter of principle, hardly ever allow the narrative
sequence to end in a condition of fragmented body but, instead,
"close" the sequence with the reestablishment of the body as a
whole. (This has made it possible for literary criticism to operate
with simple models of narrative.) Therefore, in fictional texts a
speaking organ is only a stable *pars pro toto* whose metonymic
stability consists in the maintenance of the relation between body
and "I"—even if the roles are reversed: the body speaks and the
"I" listens. The enunciation remains stable.

Naturally, it is not just because of these apparent similarities
between schizophrenic and fictional texts that many comparisons
have been drawn between them in connection with the thematizations of the body's organs and the assignment of enunciation
functions to the organs (e.g., in pornographic fiction the sexual
organs can think and speak).[4] Also the relative disintegration
of language (not least in poetry), that is, the various forms of
violation of normal syntax and semantics have been stressed as
significant points of similarity. Finally, the special presentation
of reality in schizophrenic texts is in many ways similar to fiction
as such; the events depicted in schizophrenic texts are often fan-
tastic and bizarre to a degree that is found only in fiction, where
anything can happen. Nevertheless, we maintain that these similarities are mostly superficial. Professional writers are seldom
psychotic or schizophrenic even though they are sometimes able
to master mental states that are reminiscent of regression or
psychosis.

THE SLIDINGS OF SIGNIFIERS IN ENUNCIATION AND DISCOURSE

The lack of a body totality is an important character of the body
fable in schizophrenic texts. The body is fragmented and can
furthermore be described as being deterritorialized, that is, with-

out a stable local identity. The deterritorialization applies not only to the imaginary body but also to speech that is deterritorialized insofar as it does not establish a space of speech with appropriate roles or character masks connected with definite socially valid matters. The fragmented imaginary body has abolished the boundaries of the territory of speech. The speaker's own body can then merge with any other body.

The Second Person in the enunciation is excluded, and the First Person disappears from the space of speech precisely because the fantasmatic body appears in the form of fragmentation. The fragmentation of the imaginary body is synonymous with an effective destruction of the deictic dynamics of the text. That is, both deictic and anaphoric references to the social reality, the topic of conversation, and the speakers, function only in an incoherent manner from the point of view of the narrative and logic of the text.

The presence of fragmentation and its acute or chronic dominance thus means that it becomes more or less impossible to establish a stable text and a stable structure of dialogue. Speech, fantasy, and reality are no longer regarded or experienced as distinct and individually identifiable elements in a coherent universe. (See Figure 5.1).

Another important characteristic of the body fable and its formation is the repetition of the elements of the fable in particular variations. In accordance with our pointing out the failure of the function of anaphora, it can be seen how these repetitions are disconnected both internally and externally. Nonetheless the repetition mechanisms in the linguistic presentation do have an effect: they may give the patient a feeling of being in a valid space of meaning where the patient has the possibility to organize and perceive himself or herself socially and to reestablish his or her plastic, imaginary body reality.

We find an example of this in the letter to the "Dear Servants" where the repetitions in the middle of the letter uphold the master-servant relationship that the letter started with. *I* (the writer of the letter) ask *you* (my servants) to do *this and that* (concerning my body).

Figure 5.1. Fragment of a drawing. Notice how the parts of the body appear to be disintegrated and permeable. Everything beneath the dotted line that divides "head" and "body" seems undefined and multiple. The drawing is, ostensibly, a self-portrait.

Note that the letter does not contain any syntactic or grammatical mistakes. The First and the Second Person in the enunciation are apparently stable, at least on the surface; they are explicitly named ("Servants" who are addressed by an "I"). On the other hand, both the "I" and the "you" have disappeared in the middle of the letter, and the direction of the letter has become diffuse; apart from "Dr. Brünnicke," it is not clear who is to carry out all these terrible operations. Nevertheless, the space of speech is preserved not least because the redundancy in the thematic field is able to give a stable quality to the patient's speech. The repetitions of the lethal and self-destructive parts of the body, supplemented by metonymically contiguous expressions (e.g., "active service," "sword," "duel"), are placed precisely at the critical point, namely where the writer has to explain the causes of his own disastrous situation ("Her mild eyes persecute me") and where a constructive suggestion has to be made.

As a message the text is rather striking: it is addressed to the writer's "Servants" but concludes with a reversal of the Second-Person receiver: "naturally I am always at your service." The receivers have now suddenly become "masters" to whose service the writer commends himself. The First Person in the enunciation of the text, its "I", has now changed its position in relation to the Second Person, as the latter has changed its character (from "servants" to "masters").

Along with these changes in the course of the text, in the middle part of the letter, as we pointed our earlier, there is a breakthrough of discursive elements with some common thematic features: "twenty stabs," "suicide," "active service," "drilled through," "crucifixion," "duel," "sawn off," "being thrown to the lions," and "boiling alive" are all elements that refer to death as a basic thematic figure. However, as discursive elements they have been taken from totally different contexts—from the Christian discourse ("crucifixion") and probably also from the cannibalistic being "boiled alive" of the comic strip. The metonymic slidings from element to element are thus semantically founded: everything mentioned is an example of one and the same semantic relation: the relationship of body and death. And through the varied repetition of the same matter, the writer of the letter may, as mentioned above, achieve a feeling of having rectified and stabilized the deictic structure and thereby the totality of the imaginary body.

Obviously, we have only sketchily analyzed the letter to the "Dear Servants." A number of the incongruities in the text—for example, that there are "mild eyes" that persecute the patient and that he therefore wants to go to a "rough place"—thus belong to thematic analysis.

By no means do all texts present repetitions and metonymic slidings of such a simple semantic nature. Many are extremely complicated. In principle, the fragmented imaginary body makes it possible for the elements of the body fable to space themselves in different ways so that all possible elements, including neologisms like "trisks" and "svilts," are connected with the fable. This often occurs in a kind of numeral structure, as exemplified below:

P.   And after all there are . . . but there the state has done very good work, they have discovered the hundred thousand millions times million three hundred things on the bottom of the Silkeborg Lakes. Crimes happen all the time on the bottom of the Silkeborg Lakes, in the Zealand Lakes and the North Sea, and up in the rainbow, they had looked up into the clouds, put into the mannequins, yes, there . . . down in, down in caves, all possible places.

I.   Has the state done all that?

P.   No, those who are interfering.

I.   Aha.

P.   And three hundred, they don't want three hundred things to be discovered, because people must not be discovered, they sp—— them, they kill people if they can.

I.   Yes.

P.   But, uh, nobody is allowed except trisks and svilts.

I.   No.

P.   But now . . . under Øster Søgade [a street in Copenhagen], there they have beated three hundred, eight, eight thousand, um, three hundred things, or one hundred, three hundred things down with sexual . . . big sexual organs, so that liver, kidney, and lungs slide out crushed. One can see down there, they are carried up day and night. And it's like that all over the country and on all plan . . . thirty planets they have done the same.

I.   Thirty planets?

P.   . . . they have, that is destroyed three hundred things, and they do the same on all planets and in private homes, if they don't get down on their knees and pray, morning and evening, and go to church, then we cannot exist.

We see again how the textual structure of the dialogue is presented in a quite special way when the deictic anchorings of the speech are altered and its manifested relations among signifiers, and its relations between sign and sentence, appear in the form of frequent substitutional metonymic slidings. Read superficially, the text does not consist of much more than chains of metonymic slidings in thematic and phonemically ordered chains of signifiers. However, the text is not meaningless. The metonymic slidings and the internal relations of the signifiers form a specific textual meaning (see Figure 5.2).

It can easily be seen how the signifiers are organized in chains. At the same time, it is obvious that each of these chains is replaceable as a sentence or text unit. We notice that the chains of signifiers of the schizophrenic patient in the interview—and thus the patient's thoughts or thought sequences—are linked together according to relatively simple principles: as repetitions; as relations of similarity or contrast; and as relations of contiguity in theme, sound, and sentence construction (the phonological and syntactic structure of the text). Sometimes prepositional terms function as triggers of the chains of signifiers, and sometimes it is a case of one chain releasing another like "rings of a necklace that is a ring in another necklace made of rings," to use Lacan's subtle formulation.[5] These relations of repetition, similarity, and contiguity, which in schizophrenia appear almost with the arbitrary systematization of a catalogue, are illustrated in the following letter:

> Dear Mother,
> I am 50 times orthodox. I am 50 times orphan and gave a cat a piece of breadd myself three times, and that is four times orphan, of the girls I paidd some gooseberries two times, that is three times orphan. I movedd a Turkidsh lady's chair two times, that is two times orphan. I paid the girl here 13–14 in 9–10 gooseberries and . . . [etc.]

Such a text seems to us interminable, since the repetitions in the chains of signifiers are not controlled by a theme organized according to the rules of a logical or narrative system. They appear to be controlled exclusively by the signifiers' relations of similarity and contiguity. Furthermore, these relations are placed within an extremely simple sentence model: subject noun phrase, verb + numeral + constituent A + constituent B. In each col-

Figure 5.2. A sketch of some of the chains of signifiers in the interview on p. 80

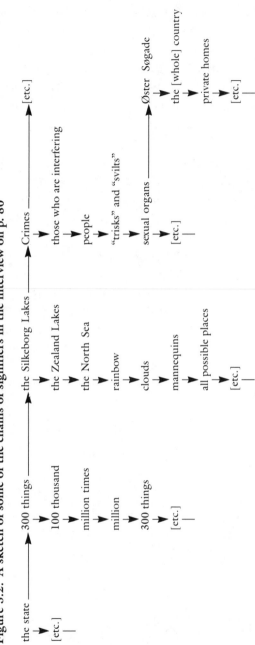

umn of the model, by constantly changing the components of the signifiers, the text rattles off a kind of catalogue that fills out reality. This is depicted in Figure 5.3.

As exemplified in Figure 5.3, the repetitions in the text take place in chains of signifiers. Everything in the text, right down to signifiers the size of a letter or a phoneme, is repeated. Notice, for example, the text's "exaggerated use of the letter d" as it says in the textbook from which we have taken the letter.[6] The *smallest segments of the text take an active part in producing the text,* as they are being transported from syntagma to syntagma by means of the metonymic slidings that characterize the whole form and appearance of schizophrenia.

Thus, we see that metonymic slidings take place on all levels of the text, even on the level of the formation of syllables and words. As we have noted, all these redundancies have the effect of giving the patient a feeling of presence (deictic structure) and thereby a feeling that the self is unified and assembled.

Figure 5.3. Schematization of the letter on p. 81 showing the relations of similarity and contiguity

I am	50	times	orthodox
I am	50	times	orphan
			and
		gave	
	a	cat	
	a		piece of breadd
myself	three	times	and
that is	four	times	orphan
the	one	girl	
I have paidd	some		gooseberries
	two	times	
that is	three	times	orphan
I have			movedd
	a		Turkidsh
		lady's	chair
	two	times	
that is	two	times	orphan
I have paidd		the girl	
here	13–14		
in	9–10		gooseberries

[etc.]

In the "orphan" text the world (*Umwelt*) is being structured, and the body (*Innenwelt*) is structured only through that. However, the *Umwelt* is merely a projection of the *Innenwelt*. The metonymic slidings and substitutions have, of course, the same function as in the previous examples: to re-create the body's non-fragmented imaginary form and to reestablish stable enunciative relations.[7]

In the interviews with the elderly lady (pp. 38–44), however, we noticed that the metonymic substitutions actually were not able to give the patient a sufficiently stable relation between the fragmented imaginary body and the Second Person present (the interviewer). The fact that the patient did not succeed in this meant that the attempts had to continue: but this also means that the patient tried to maintain the relatively stable relations among the fantasms of the fragmented body and speech as a whole. Speech had always to deal with the body.

This is seen frequently in schizophrenic patients. The speech about the body—the body fables—occurs as slidings of a metonymic kind between the signifiers through the registers of enunciation and discourse. It is the *relation* between the two processes of sliding in enunciation and discourse that constitutes what we shall call the logical structure of the imaginary body. The imaginary body exists and functions as a signifying process in the speaker, determined by the signifiers' usual ways of being organized, that is, in accordance with what in grammer is called *syntactic forms*. Even though the signifiers of the imaginary body are not necessarily structured according to normal linguistic rules of syntax in the same way that speech defined by enunciation is structured, we still use the concept of syntax to define the interrelationships of the signifiers in the unconscious processes that form the imaginary body. This is because we think that speech in the discursive register does not differ fundamentally from the speech that can be heard directly in enunciation.[8]

There is a basic assumption to the effect that the imaginary body is formed through the relation between the signifiers and that it therefore does not exist as "content" or "meaning" before the appearance of the signifiers. This point of view is essential in attempting to understand the pathogenic factors of schizophrenia.

The French psychoanalyst Lemaire writes that the unconscious is elementarily composed of signifiers or groups of signifiers "which later enter into the composition of words and then into the composition of *unconscious fantasies* whose overall construction constitutes those unconscious strata which are more accessible to analysis."[9] It is, therefore, a mistake to imagine that the unconscious contains some special, hidden meaning of one kind or another.

We shall show in the next chapter that a more precise definition of body fantasms and their status as signifiers requires an analysis of the imaginary body as a splitting between body proper and body of the other. This splitting functions in specific ways in connection with the distribution of the signifiers. These specific ways have to do with the subject's *desire*. Different kinds of desire make for different kinds of texts and enunciative relations. Without the concept of desire, we cannot understand the patients' complex and often ambivalent ways of expressing emotional phenomena—their anxiety, hate, affection, pleasure, and their emotional attachments to their families, fellow patients, and therapists.

CHAPTER SIX

THE DYNAMICS OF BODY AND FANTASY

BODY PROPER AND BODY OF THE OTHER

In this chapter we shall try to identify the dynamics of the imaginary body. We shall further isolate this complicated area by putting forward the view that fantasy is a structure, the elements of which can neither be "passively" combined with other elements nor be composed and structured in an endless number of accidental or arbitrary ways. Fantasy exists and functions by virtue of the effects of its elements. These effects are produced by the fantasms being repeated, wiped out, formed, and re-formed in particular patterns in accordance with particular principles and laws.

In the preceding chapters we have attempted to show how this happens through the interplay of signifiers in various schizophrenic texts. When analyzing the letters and interviews, we described the ways in which the fantasms appeared as joints and as metonymic slidings of the signifiers in schizophrenic texts, and how these joints and slidings had a determining effect on the patients' imagination. At the same time we described the way in which the activity of the fantasms affects the communicative ability of the speaker. We noted how the different thematic structures in the speech—among them themes that dealt with the body and its organs—were repeated word for word or in slightly altered forms and, in other cases, were radically changed and replaced by other themes. In this connection we established that these repetitions and alterations could be more precisely determined by analyses of the processes of the signifiers that take place in the two registers of speech. In psychoanalytic literature, investigations have been carried out, not just of the form and content of the repetitions, but also of their nature.

The possible existence of a *repetition compulsion* has been put forward, and it has been emphasized that this repetition compulsion is basic to an analysis and understanding of the psychic apparatus and its way of functioning.[1] Thus, the repetition compulsion has been characterized as the mechanism that causes the continually returning rhythmic appearance of the symptoms in the unconscious, contrary to the wishes and the will of the patient.

Even if it may seem reasonable to assume that the repetition compulsion exists, however, more theoretical work must be done in order to link this concept to a number of other necessary concepts with which it is intimately associated. In the following pages we shall give a brief account of some of these concepts, which on the one hand are important analytical tools for the understanding of the dynamics of schizophrenic speech, and that on the other hand play a part in the formation of a topological model in which the problem of repetition can be placed. The poles of this topological model are the *body proper* and *the body of the other.*

The body proper and the body other are nonreducible contrasts in the topological model. They constitute different positions in the same structure, positions that can never identify or merge. From the point of view of the topological model, they can only "approach" one another and "distance themselves" from one another asymptotically.[2] The effect of this noneffaceable distance between the body proper and the body of the other is a just as noneffaceable aggressive tension between the two positions, and thus an equally noneffaceable binding together of them.

DEVELOPMENT OF FANTASY

The historical starting point for the use of the concepts of body proper and body of the other belongs to the discussion of early psychogenesis. This period in the life of the human being was regarded as being decisive for the individual as far as the formation of the imaginary body (its structure, stability) and its prospects for further development were concerned. The final structured form of the body had to be determined in psychogenesis. It was likewise here that the energetics of the body fantasms were established, that is, their changes, transitional forms, and standstills. The results of psychogenesis were described in psychiatry in such terms as "character trait," "ego strength," "ego weakness," and the ability of the ego to "integrate" and "adapt."

In the case of early psychogenesis, in primary socialization, the body of the other can be understood as the incorporated mirror image of the infant, the child, that is, as exclusively fantasmatic reflections about the other.[3] In preverbal communication with parents, siblings, and others, these early notions function as a matrix that determines the psychomotoric development of the child but that has little significance if no responses are given to the child's communicative gestures.

In this early period, the body of the other functions as the fantasmatic basis of an adaptive and gestalting sensory perception. Without this basis there would be no real interaction between the child and his or her surroundings. The impressions that characterize early experience leave a kind of pictorial writing in the child in the form of traces. These inscriptions produce meaning insofar as they are the cause of systems of differences.

The body of the other can similarly be understood as the place where these differences are systematized. It is the body of the other that is the matrix of all subsequent internalizations and identifications. The body of the other is the place where psychomotoric coordination is anticipated, and it is through the body of the other that the ego is contrastively formed, by comparing itself with the other, making an impression on and trying to dominate the other, and so forth. In other words, the body of the other is the field that developmental psychology investigates for the early cognitive and creative development of the child.

In the further processes of socialization the acquisition of language and the repression of the Oedipus complex have important roles to play.[4] Through these two mental events the body of the other still functions, but now retroactively on a fantasmatic and identificational basis, that is, as a *socially determined imaginary structure.*

In attempting to understand the body proper, it is important to note its function in relation to the body of the other. The body proper is a *spacing,* that is, a dividing and articulating principle for the organization of fantasms.[5] The body proper directs the fantasms to follow certain syntactic patterns and to enter into certain internal relations, patterns, and relations that cut out, postpone, or repeat the fantasms that, in the shape of signifiers, form the imaginary body (see Chapter 5). But the body proper does not merely space the fantasms and their mutual relations; it is, at the same time, able to disorganize and obliterate them. In other words, the body proper is secondary in relation to the body of the other.

In psychoanalytic theory, the activity of the body proper is of a specific nature; it constitutes aggressive intentions.[6] And it determines, broadly speaking, the fantasms' possibilities of replacing, transforming, and linking together. Thus, aggressivity is the essential force in the restructurings of fantasms. It must be seen in the context of the existence of a *constant desire to obliterate the discordance between the body proper and the body of the other.* This discordance—the discrepancy between the two bodies—is, however, the condition for the constitution of fantasy.[7] Without this discrepancy fantasy would not exist at all. Fantasy is a drama that is played out between the body proper and the body of the other.

FANTASY AND REALITY

Against the background of these very brief descriptions of the processes of early psychogenesis, we can clarify our conception of compulsory repetition, the concept that was the starting point for the introduction of the concepts of body proper and body of the other. The relationship between body proper and body of the

other is subject to the desire to unite the body proper with the
body of the other and to make the desire for the other equal to
the incorporation and conquering of the other. But precisely because it is impossible to satisfy this desire, the activity of the
fantasms never ceases. And this again means that the signifiers on
the level of the discursive register must constantly be repeated
and postponed, restructured and transformed. Through this the
real subjectivity of the individual is formed (see Chapter 2).

The body proper and the body of the other together constitute
a structure that anchors the speaker to the ways in which the
fantasms manifest themselves in the concrete everyday conversation situation. This includes situations where the addressee—the
other—is present only in an imagined form. In thought and
speech the fantasmatic elements relate to one another in a
number of different ways, depending on the events, influences,
and ways of being with other people, and possibilities of identification that the individual has experienced.

On another level it can be said that fantasms in speech and
thought depend on the individual discursive adaptation of signifiers. For example, shifts, dislocations, or breaks in the structuring of the signifiers can occur so that it becomes possible to
distinguish different forms of fantasy activity qualitatively. Psychoanalytic definitions of "psychosis," "neurosis," and "perver-
sion" are thus classifications of such different forms of discursive
structurings of fantasms. But let us attempt to describe more
precisely how the topological model of the body proper and the
body of the other achieves direct importance in the construction
of the form and content of schizophrenic speech. A schizophrenic patient once imagined that her body was organized in the
following way:

P. They tear everything to pieces. With their big sexual organs.
    Yes. They do that all over the earth, if you don't get down on
    your knees to pray, morning and evening and attend church
    then it happens, the same thing can happen to you.
I. It sounds as if the sexual organs persecute these people.
P. No, after all it's trisks and svilts, they have very big . . . they

have, not all of them have, but they have very big sexual organs.

I. Hm.

P. And they *want* to knock people down, and *want* to do things like that.

I. And they do it?

P. It interests them, yes.

I. With their sexual organs?

P. Both the ladies who have lain, a lady came up who definitely wanted to have something to do with that . . . kind of thing, it lies, they get a terrible p——, a terrible punishment, they burn, that coal for millions of billions of years, they become completely black, and they get pains inside when the fire reaches into the insides, and scream and . . . they get pains and a mare . . . a terribly severe punishment. They are lying down there with their big sexual organs under Øster Søgade [a street in Copenhagen]. Invisible.

I. One can see them a bit?

P. Well, I can't see them, but the vicar's wives can see them.

I. They have seen them?

P. And with all the young people, the various ones who can see . . .

I. You were talking before about some machines?

P. Yes, there are machines on . . .

I. Is there any connection between the sexual organs and the machines?

P. No, because the machines were supposed to help them and the earth so that we could exist better, can exist better.

I. Hm. This perspective spirit which . . .

P. Yes?

I. . . . you mentioned before?

P. Yes, we all have perspectives, everyone does, and then you ask the perspective spirit to help you find a home you can live in, if you don't have one, and so . . .

I. Where is this perspective spirit?

P. Yes, where is it? As a rule one has four perspectives, one in the head and one in each wrist, yes.

I. And what happened to the fourth?

P. One in the head . . . no, I don't really know. Or two in the head. . . . There is at any rate, I don't really remember. But I, I don't rightly know it's arranged, I don't know how it's arranged.

I. This perspective spirit?

P. Yes, there is a . . . everything, everything has a spirit, every-thing has a meaning, and there is a meaning, a spirit which belongs to the perspective, there is a, an excellent spirit. And they can help to find a, a friendly home for one.

I. But is it a part of the religion?

P. No, it's ordinary things that happen, ordinary, nothing to do with religion.

I. Have you asked this perspective spirit for help?

P. No, I haven't. It's only our people.

I. Our people?

P. That is all who are put in. All those who are put into the body. . . . I don't know how they are put . . . they have been in the arms before, now they have slid, the arms, they are not in the arms now, they have also been in the legs, and the thighs, they have slid out now, I don't think there are any in the thighs, no, they have slid out. And, um, they have been separated and slid out. Yes.

I. Do you think that *I* am a person or do *I* also have a skin on me?

P. Yes, I can't see that, but the ladies can. Yes, yes. You *are* a person.

I. Hm.

P. But we all have skins. We all have skin, or what should I say, we have skin, or . . . yes, we have . . .

I. That's true enough.

P. Yes, we have.

I. Yes. Am I also influenced by all these trisks and svilts which you . . . ?

P. Well, I don't know. I don't know how your life has been; it could be that you have been maltreated, both in your work and . . . you haven't been able to find a home and, I don't know, things like that, it could be so many things. And they try to stop one from getting . . . yes, I can't say, there are no limits to what can happen to people from that side.

I. I think that you have quite macabre thoughts.

P. Well, it's not thoughts, it's something real.

I. It's something real?

P. Yes it is. One can investigate it and see of it's true.

It is probably apparent that the interviewer is trying to deter-mine the relation of the patient's discursive register to the socially given discourses that the patient touches on in various ways. In a good hermeneutic manner, the interviewer tries to connect two important functions. On the one hand there are some fantasmatic figures that the patient constantly talks about, "the perspective spirit" and many other parts of the fragmented body, and different socially recognized fictional themes belonging to the discourse (e.g., religion, the apocalyptic fable). On the other hand, there is reality in the form of the reality of the conversation that is taking place here and now in the time and space of the enunciation.

This happens not least in the form of consolidating questions like "Do you think I am a person or do I also have a skin on me?" "Am I also influenced by all these trisks and svilts?"; and "Where is this perspective spirit?" But at no point in the dialogue does the patient try to establish a textually stable relationship among fantasy, fictional themes, and reality in such a way that her speech can at all be linked to reality here and now. Apparently the patient neither can nor will give a clear account of the relation between the fabulous global incidents in her speech and the socially existing reality. The interviewers' attempt to understand the patient—his efforts to achieve insight into the other—fail completely, and the interview as a whole bears the clear mark of the patient's lack of respect or consideration for the time, space, and persons of social reality.

What is obviously lacking is fixed roles and functions linked to the individual, among them the wish to show sympathetic understanding, to mix socially, to achieve mutual understanding and cooperation. It is not easy to come to grips with the interviewer, for example, concerning his interest in everything the patient relates. All the same, there is a certain degree of formal contact. The interviewer's questions are promptly answered; the patient is not reluctant and does not try to interrupt the interviewer.

As we established in Chapter 3, in connection with another interview, the different spaces of the speech are disorganized. We described, furthermore, how the use of various forms of deixis placed the speaker in relation to different spaces: a space of real-

ity, a space of speech and finally a logical space linked to the
discourse involved. We established that the individual's speech
affixes the discourse to the space of reality and the space of conversation as the discourse imparts to these spaces a number of
points of anchorage in an ideologically meaningful context.

In the interview we can see that the patient is unable to establish the logical space of speech in the from of a stable linking
together of the space of conversation and the space of reality.
Actually, interviewer and patient cannot be understood as being
anchored in the same social context. The participants, time, and
space in the interview and the placing of the participants are only
vaguely identified. As a consequence, the patient's speech does
not present any social reality. On the other hand, a kind of repair-
ing maneuver can be seen in the interview as a whole, as compen-
sation for the lack of social reality.

Everything that has been rejected or is absent from the logical
space of speech that the patient's speech nevertheless tries to refer
to is present in the patient's fantasmatic organization of her
speech. It appears as material that recurs in scenes in an imaginary world that constitutes reality for the patient. The imaginarily structured universe—the patient's fable about the sexual
organs, the perspective spirit, the "trisks and svilts"—becomes an
imaginarily structured compensatory reality for the reality that
normally is *symbolically* structured and that is in principle not
only determined by the projections, the subjective feelings, and
the fantasies of the individual but that is also socially defined and
recognized. "It's not thoughts, it's something real," the patient
says, admittedly about the content of her thought universe, in
that she invokes a reality that cannot be said to be socially and
culturally codified. But, at the same time, she invites verification
of her claims: "one" can investigate it and see if it is true; "I"
don't know; "I" cannot see it; and so on. In other words, the
patient comments on her own speech. "The patient's comments
on her unintelligible remark have the value of an analysis, for they
contain the equivalent of the remark expressed in a generally
comprehensible form," writes Freud in connection with a patient

in the first stages of schizophrenia.[8] He also writes that these comments "throw light at the same time on the meaning and the genesis of schizophrenic word-formation." It is this meaning we are trying to decipher here.

DELUSIONS AND PROJECTION

When the *fantasmatic scenario*—determined by the imaginary structure of the signifier—replaces first the deictically conditioned relation of speech and reality and, second, the relationship of speaker and addressee that is determined by enunciation, then what psychiatry calls *delusions* sometimes appear.

Projection is one of the primary mechanisms in the formation of delusions.[9] Projective mechanisms appear in speech when linguistic elements are exposed to certain transformations. For example, half or whole sentences, thematic sequences, single words, syllables, and letters can be the objects of different forms of changes and inversions, or negations—of the subject and object of the sentence, of active and passive forms, and the like. In his analysis of the autobiography of Schreber, Freud gives a famous example of such a projective mechanism. "It is a remarkable fact," writes Freud, "that the familiar principal forms of paranoia can all be represented as contradictions of the single proposition: 'I (a man) *love him* (a man).'" Thus, the sentence "I love him" is transformed in the delusions of paranoia partly by a negation and a permutation of the verb ("I do not *love* him—I *hate* him"), partly by exchanging the subject of the sentence with the object and, vice versa, "by *projection* into another one," as Freud says.[10] ("*He hates* [persecutes] *me,* which will justify me in hating him.") These transformations finally produce the paranoiac's consciousness of not loving but rather hating others, because these others persecute him. Freud accounts in the same way for the transformations of erotomania: first the transformation "I do not love *him*—I love *her*"; next the changing of this sentence by projection into "I observe that *she* loves me" or, more directly, "I do

not love *him*—I love *her,* because *she loves me.*" As regards paranoid jealousy, the result of the transformation is for men: "It is
not *I* who love the man—*she* loves him" and similarly for women:
"It is not *I* who love the women—*he* loves them." Freud sees the
fourth possibility of transformation in megalomania, where the
transformations take the following form: "*I do not love at all—I do
not love anyone,*" which is equivalent to "I love myself."

Projection is a basic mechanism in the psychogenetic development of the child. Projection is stabilized in the final phases of
psychogenesis, that is, in the closing phase of primary socialization. It is at this stage that the individual acquires the ability
to *symbolize.* In his life together with other people, in the conversational relations of everyday life, and so forth the child can
now symbolize everything that he or she previously could not
know or be and that he or she therefore had to project into the
surroundings.

In other words, in the early phase of socialization the distinction between the outer and the inner was unstable (e.g., the small
child who cries when his or her friend is beaten). In the final
phases of primary socialization the child is able to make the
distinction: that which is projected is now symbolized as the
child's *own* thoughts and feelings vis-à-vis the others (e.g., parents, friends, enemies) and their thoughts and feelings.

In projection the fantasmatic elements are experienced as if they
were only external, "coming from outside," in short, *something*—
things, people, relations, events—directed toward one's body but
not primarily related to the *Innenwelt.* What happens is that one
or more textual elements form a kind of mirror for the existence
of the subject.[11] It is characteristic of schizophrenia that the textually structuring function of the elements appear to be detached
from, only metonymically attached to, the larger corpus of socially functioning textuality that we call discourse. The elements
that are exposed to projection are not anchored to the instances
of the enunciation. What they lack, first and foremost, is any
anchoring to the Second Person in enunciation.

The long excerpt from the interview serves to illustrate how the

projective mechanisms function in different ways in schizophrenic speech. One notices first of all that there is an irrevocable
separation between speech and body. The body no longer carries
the patient's speech but instead—in a fragmented form—behaves
like several different, existing but foreign bodies that have independent aims. At any rate, this is how the schizophrenic sees it.
The "perspective spirit" that helps one to find a home is such a
foreign body. For whom does the perspective spirit find a home?
How? The patient answers, "For our people," that is, for "all of
those who have been put into the body." At the same time the
perspective spirit is located in the body, in the head, in each wrist,
and in a fourth place that has apparently disappeared and is unmentionable. The foreign body is double-anchored, the external
and the internal have collided, and the speech, what the speech
refers to, and the body, as three otherwise differentiated registers,
no longer cohere for the patient. They merge almost totally:

P. Yes we all have perspectives, everyone does, and then you ask
the perspective spirit to help you find a home you can live in,
if you don't have one, and so . . .
I. Where is this perspective spirit?
P. Yes, where is it? As a rule one has four perspectives, one in the
head and one in each wrist, yes.

The textually unstable relationship among fantasy, discourse, and
reality means for the patient an alienation on the level of body: a
fragmentation and a *projection*. What is rejected and projected
from the unconscious returns toward the body as reality, where it
appears as a nonintegrated signifier metonymically related to another signifier, that is, the fable of the perspective spirit.

The dichotomy between body and speech corresponds to the
split between the usual First and Second Persons, on the one
hand, and a kind of "multiplied sender" of the speech on the
other hand. In the interview these changes are rung on an "I" and
a "we," between a "tape" and "people" who "have been put into a
skin." In this way the contact between the First and Second
Persons in the enunciation (i.e., patient and interviewer) and the

speaker's desire to articulate and formulate herself in the dialogue are separated. The patient is not backed up by her self, and the First Person in the enunciation disappears from time to time. It is this split that the subject "closes" by summoning certain symbols in order to organize them where discourse appears and is mediated in the speaker: namely in the relationship of *the Other and the other*. But the schizophrenic does not succeed in "closing" the split between the staged instances of the enunciation and the other elements of the discursive register. The split remains, by and large, open and the *other speech* is "spread out" over the whole enunciation.

In a *nonpsychotic* condition this system of different terms ("I," "we," "that skin," etc.) would function with the aid of explicit or implicit references to the individual's self. Under these normal conditions the self would serve as the fixed point or as a kind of space of identity, that is, as a deeper lying truth about the speech that secures itself under different stable facades in the enunciation, in contrast to schizophrenia's throng of First-, Second- and Third-Person instances. When the nonpsychotic person uses the "I" to point to something in his or her own person as the place of intention and truth, then he or she is at the same time pointing to conscious and unconscious parts of the imaginary body, to which no truth is connected. The self exists in the "I" or in the "I's" place in enunciation. In Chapter 5 we noted how this self was a place in speech that one could point to; for example, in the expressions of love of everyday life, or popular literature ("My heart beats for you only," etc.). We then connected these imago formations with the body of the other. These references in speech to the body of the other usually work satisfactorily for the nonpsychotic person: the reference functions normally without any danger of dislocating the representation of reality. In the nonpsychotic person, the reference functions by means of *repression*. There we find a stable anchoring of speech to a repression of the whole structure of the body proper and the body of the other. Linguistic references to the abstract self—as, for example, in the statement "I know myself well enough to know that . . ."—in the nonpsychotic person is a stable reference based on the fact that the speaker has sacrificed or has had to sacrifice the fantasy about complete satisfaction of the desires of the persons around him or her and his or her own built-in instances. This sacrifice stabilizes speech. The desire of the Other can never be completely satisfied, and it is the function of speech to supplement this impossibility, this lack (manque).

FORECLOSURE AND THE IMAGINARY BODY

Let us summarize our view of nonpsychotic speech. In such speech a self-conscious I presents its linguistically covered body of the other to the other, to the Second Person of the enunciation. The linguistic substitution takes place on the basis of a repression and fixation of the body proper–body of the other structure as a whole to the unconscious, that is, to the discursive register. The body proper and the body of the other are discursive and therefore are also social, insofar as it is through discourse that the individual achieves subjectivity (different societies have different body proper–body of the other structures).

The immediate effects of repression consist in the strengthening of the stability of the relationship of the enunciation's First and Second Persons. In this way the speaker is equipped with the prerequisites for the ability to create a *space of speech* linguistically. Naturally, in the last instance language learning aims at the speaker's establishing a *logical space,* above and beyond the establishment of a space of reality and a space of speech. It is only by so doing that the connection between the Other of the discursive register and the Second Person in the enunciation—the other—is secured. This view is presented in Table 6.1.

We stated earlier that the schizophrenic's body fables function in the form of slidings of signifiers in and from the registers of discourse and enunciation. However, the repression of the body proper–body of the other structure and the decisive stable relationships between the Other of the discursive register and the

Table 6.1. The imaginary body in normal discourse and enunciation

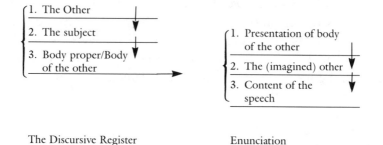

The Discursive Register   Enunciation

Second Person in the register of enunciation are not sufficiently explained by the existence of slidings of signifiers. How do the slidings of the two registers come into being? Why are there slidings between the two registers?

In posing these questions, we are entering an area of great disagreement. This concerns the etiology of schizophrenia, the earliest factors connected with the formation of schizophrenia. It is impossible here to present an even barely adequate account of this. We shall briefly sketch Jacques Lacan's view of the earliest bases of schizophrenia, which can be worked into the conceptual system we are operating with here.

However, we must point out that Lacan by no means attempts to offer a comprehensive definition of schizophrenia. He stipulates a *logical basis* of schizophrenia. This is why Lacan's theory deals less with the adult schizophrenic and more with the necessary preconditions of psychosis.

Lacan connects the repression of the body proper–body of the other structure in nonpsychotic persons with the status of the signifiers in the psychic apparatus. In order to be able to maintain the stability in speech brought about by the repression of the body proper–body of the other structure, the signifiers that enter into stable speech are *overdetermined*. They are, as it were, subjected to *a signifier of the signifiers*.[12] To Lacan the unconscious symbolic instance that determines the circulation of signifiers in the two registers of speech consists of such primary or *original signifiers*. We shall not undertake further discussions about the foundation and origin of these signifiers: we merely note that some analysts refer to them as *phallos*. A primary signifier of the signifiers is often characterized as phallic because it must be assumed that the acquisition of language—which has as its basis this original signifier—takes place under conditions of conflict where the small child loses his or her immediate reflection with the mother and instead sees him- or herself as subject to the father. Lacan says that the child learns to symbolize only when the symbolic laws of the father threaten the child's imaginary, infantile existence. The foundation of this symbolic law, the *Name-of-the-Father*, contradicts the child's wish to *be* the (mother's) *phallos*: from now on *phallos* is something the child can *have* or *lose*. The desire to absolutely and completely *be phallos* is transformed in such a way that it can be satisfied only through the symbolic functions of language. Thus, in Lacan the signifier of the signifiers is the *Name-of-the-Father*, as it is the father who *has phallos*.

We hope that we shall be forgiven this brief and therefore difficult account of the crucial processes in the child's development as Lacan describes them. However, we can now define some basic aspects of schizophrenia. The speech of the schizophrenic is characterized by a lack in the organization of the relation of the *Name-of-the-Father* and the chain of speech.[13] The relationship between the Other and the Second Person in enunciation has been disturbed and dislocated. The signifier of the signifiers is missing from the position from which it should have held the net of chains of signifiers together. As the repression of the body proper–body of the other structure is already connected with the functions of the rank-and-file signifiers, in schizophrenia the signifier of the signifiers must have become the object of a kind of prerepression. Lacan says here that psychosis is characterized by the specific process whereby the signifier of the signifiers is rejected or *foreclosed*. The *Name-of-the-Father* is excluded from the symbolic. To Lacan, the circumstance that is largely responsible for psychosis is "an accident in the register (of the signifiers) and in what takes place in it, namely the foreclosure of the Name-of-the-Father" in the place of the Other and the "failure of the paternal metaphor" that arises from this. Lacan further defines the conditions for schizophrenic development by the fact that "the Name-of-the-Father, *verworfen,* foreclosed, that is to say never having attained the place of the Other, [must] be called into symbolic opposition to the subject. It is the lack of the Name-of-the-Father in that place which, by the hole that it opens up in the signified, sets off the cascade of re-shapings of the signifier from which the increasing disaster of the imaginary proceeds, to the point at which the level is reached at which signifier and signified are stabilized in delusional metaphor."

The psychoanalyst J. Laplanche and the philosopher J.-B. Pontalis, writing about the precluded Name-of-the-Father, say that, in contrast to the mechanisms of repression, it "is not integrated into the subject's unconscious" and therefore does not return from the interior (*Innenwelt*) of the subject, but that what is foreclosed on the contrary "re-emerges in the 'Real' particularly through the phenomenon of hallucination."[14] For the schizophrenic patient, the foreclosed *Name-of-the-Father*—in the form of several representatives—exists and is very real. It is a tape that's speaking on behalf of the patient.

The way the patient in the interview, when referring to herself and her own person, uses elements like "I," "we," "that skin," "people," "the ladies," "tape," and so on points to the fact that the patient's perception and understanding of her "I" consists in a kind of reflection of the behavior, experiences, and language of others. All in all, the patient's "I" appears as a linguistic element equal to all possible other elements and not as a specific word that refers to a well-defined and socially designed identity. The imaginary body is, of course, linguistically articulated in the interview. After all, the patient uses language symbolically in that she addresses the interviewer and explains her many problems. But, in contrast to nonpsychotic speech, the articulation does not function *representationally*; it does not function as symbols for the not fully controllable relation of the *body of the other and the*

other who is being spoken to. This division of the subjective body
of the other and the other who is addressed in enunciation, the
Second Person, is pervasive for the schizophrenic. The patient
does not control the representation of the body of the other; it is
split and its representation fades. This is one of the insistent
effects of the projection on the patient's speech.

When the body of the other as imaginary structure is fragmented, the individual's interaction with his or her fellow human
beings is made difficult or even impossible. The body of the other
is split and fragmented in a specific way however. The fantasms,
cathected with pleasure or displeasure, which the body of the
other consists of and that the patient's speech constantly repro-
duces, continuously gives the patient an opportunity to talk
about herself and her fantasies. At the same time, these fantasms
are being rejected as belonging to the speaker herself: they represent the self as nonexistent. The body of the other thus is not a
part of the patient's self but exists outside, in the external world.
It is outside the body that the body of the other plays its menac-
ing roles in the patient's life. Public life, newspapers, radio and
television programs, magazines, and so forth all become threatening, and the patient's relationship to them is one of disavowal.
We could say that the body of the other has lost its subjectivity; it
has become foreign, a partial object in the discourse of the surrounding world. The patient answers the question, "What do *you*
do at home?" with "Well, now *they've* got *Berlingske Tidende* [a
well-known Danish newspaper], so I read *Berlingske Tidende*
aloud. There are twenty from different planets who listen to it,
and one from this planet who listens to it, and if there is anything
which must . . . ," and so on. On the one side is language, on the
other is body, but to the patient body and language are neither
logically nor sexually connected or united.

In the next chapter we shall explore the way the body of the
other loses its subjectivity. With a view to the therapeutic possibilities, we shall discuss to what extent various given power
relations in the dialogue (especially between patient and therapist)
are of importance for the functions of the imaginary body.

CHAPTER SEVEN

RECONSTRUCTION OF REALITY IN SCHIZOPHRENIA

REPAIR MANEUVERS IN LANGUAGE

In the previous chapters we described some of the processes that underlie the manifold ways in which schizophrenic persons think and express themselves. It has been our constant endeavor to take their own utterances as our starting point and to subject them to thorough analysis in order to gain an understanding of, and an insight into, *the reality of schizophrenia.*

We can sum up very briefly how, in our view, schizophrenic reality is experienced and how it is constantly being reconstructed in the everyday lives of many people. First and foremost, schizophrenic speech and writing display a number of features that on the surface impede normal communication. These features all point to the crucial function of enunciation in the production of text—including, or course, its function in connection with those processes of a linguistic nature that are termed "thinking" and "thoughts." In the speech of schizophrenics—in contrast to that of neurotics—the instances of the enunciation begin to get blurred; as a conversation partner one begins to doubt who is saying what, and to whom the speech is addressed. The schizophrenic text is marked by instability of the instances in the enunciation, and as a consequence temporality, spatiality, and elements relating to the persons appear to be replaceable: time, place, persons, and objects referred to in speech are subject to constant substitutions, often governed by similarity and contiguity of the signifiers, on which the workings of the psychic apparatus rest. At the same time, there are expressions in schizophrenic texts that indicate that these changes in the registers of speech are closely related to changes in the experience of the body; the changes in the enunciation processes are thus connected with changes in the speaker's imaginary body. (See Figure 7.1).

⌐There are many indications that there is a direct link between the place of speech—the I / You / Here / Now system that organizes the enunciation—and the articulation of the imaginary body. In states of schizophrenia, the place of speech appears unstable and diffuse, corresponding to an experience of the body as fragmented, nondelimitable, and partial. As a result of these changes, the otherwise relatively firm boundary between internal and external, between self and surroundings, has gradually become penetrable. Here and Now tend toward the infinite; local matters merge with global; and the speaker takes on the disguises of the multitude of figures made available by the discourses that come to hand. From now on fantasy governs speech. Any physically present conversation partner seems alternately to recede from, and reenter into, the semantic space that the speech establishes.⌐The signifier exercises control over the content. Language

Figure 7.1. Letter written by a schizophrenic patient. Note that time stands still: "last week's" and "the week before that" are frozen in the present tense. Likewise, it is not possible to ask the "Chief Doctor" for his "full name."

Last week's mistakes will, as I understand, always be corrected, but is not always that the mistakes of the week before that are corrected. The materials have not arrived yet, but I assume that they will arrive during the afternoon. My mistakes are many, but that does not matter, for they have been corrected. It is absolutely no use for me to file a complaint when it is not written correctly. and signed by the Chief Doctor, whose full name I do not know as I have never asked him about it.

Yours, with the highest regard,
[signature]

has achieved independence. One patient explained it in the following way:[1]

    I.   What did you say?

    P.   In lewd words.

    I.   What did you say?

    P.   I have the phonetic transcription put in with lewd words, so I have had to manage postal service myself.

    I.   Hm.

    P.   This is how you can end up. My brother running about dead, wrong in photography and running around in the brainwash psychic research . . . Lewd words are put in.

    I.   Who brought lewd words into you?

    P.   It is Spain which delivers.

    I.   Hm.

    P.   That is the way the mothers have behaved in Spain obscenely.

    I.   Hm.

    P.   On the beach in night life, in, in, in night clubs and such like the decent mother's life which hasn't understood that they belong with the festive church life.

    I.   Hm.

    P.   And not to death's cleaning squad, who clean up every day in a sunset, eternal . . . and prostituted. The mothers I only clean after death, and then they have behaved so obscenely all over Europe, and it is then that they get a beating and they have been unable to get them to listen over the hearing ring.

    I.   Hm.

    P.   From Spain. It is Spain that does the serving. Also in the lavatories there is lesbian phonetic transcription, in cafeterias and public lavatories. In that way serving is done over the photographic life until it is coal-cellar clean below.

    I.   Yes.

    P.   It is the Russians, cleaned public lavatories for me for the time being, later I will do a cleaning for the Russians. They can manage that part of the cellar. It's called the ballet "Swan Lake."

As can easily be observed, certain parts of the patient's body, and the functions of the body, seem to exist in a different place from the physical body in the real space of speech: the "phonetic transcription," which has been "put in" and that controls the meaning of the speech is invariably being delivered in Spain or from

Spain. "The mothers" have "behaved in Spain obscenely," and the "lesbian phonetic transcription" pervades everything. But all in all we must conclude that the patient's speech—in the form of this "phonetic transcription"—functions outside the communicative community (the "hearing ring" mentioned by the patient) that the patient and her surroundings constitute. On the one hand, the speaker is present here, in the conversational space; on the other hand, she is at one and the same time present somewhere else, that is, where is "My brother running about dead, wrong in photography."

At the same time that the patient gives expression to her experience of these transitivistic splitting processes, her text also bears the mark of huge repair maneuvers. In the lives of many patients, these efforts seem to be grand projects, "government task" or memberships of "death's cleaning squad," which as it appears maintains order throughout Europe. Many patients thus assume responsibility for the global or cosmic order. In Chapter 1 we presented two letters written by a patient whose entire life seemed to be governed by such global projects. This is reflected among other things in the names of the addressees appearing on two of the letters she wrote: "The American Police" and "Berlin's and Madrid's Police". Let us consider yet another of these letters.[2] (Note: The letter was not written by the same patient who was interviewed above.)

Sankt Hans Hospital,
Jan. 26, 19——

To Emperor
Must Lie In bed during the day
Could we please have a little influence here.
Have paid state and municipality. All the patients in the countryside are ill, and we dare not say that we know N. N. [the patient's name] is bringing decadences home. The police. Living people who want monster, can buy a felt mask Theodor Thorngren, I have got one, you only feel a splash in the deep water and long hair can be stuck on the frock, or the latter is in folds from the yoke at the back. May America get the letter. Must have an operation we say about all decadences in order that they are not blind, and in order to see the animal inside, some have eaten a human. It is probably equally against us, but isn't it necessarily us. Because it is. And even 12 each. Quickly. They have a knot at the back. Must the decadences be

married in order to have an operation. We ask here to be spared that
nonsense, they are all ill, and must catch you a monster. 30 Monsters and
an acetic acid balloon. Chamber pots required when we are in bed. No
intercourse. Must not be married if it is the rest of us. Not until towards
the day 9 if there's no hurry lying down. It has been said in the 19th of
January, and we think we hear in the concentration 1 month 19th of
February, as the police don't talk to us. Rye bread lasts to all eternity.
Sankt Hans Hospital is in Roskilde. They say courthouse and police
station are not ours. It has been here reported. Must catch monster must
now be said, whether they are to marry or *not*. When we are in bed the
police can have the frocks, one is enough to take unto *America*. Want to be
married, work before and after the operations. Also the men's hospital the
frocks are for catching monsters in. And old bedsheets to insert at the
back. All over the world. By N. N. I have taken over the government in
Berlin. *Germany is Danish*. and the adjoining provinces. The nurses are
now from Spain as it is said they drink down there. I N. N.

                                                    Am the government
in Berlin and it is for the record.
Want war in Rio de Joneira
I Berlin take the radio

                                out of the houses
                                catch monsters
Decadences are strongly referred to the imperial palaces in order to take
100 murders of and under 100, if you please, others referred the place.

                                                    Refuted in the police
for cure.

                                The paupers.

As in the interview sequence just quoted, we can observe how
the First Person in the enunciation seems to be divided into at
least two locatable spaces: one a sort of domestic space, characterized by a careful mention of place and time ("Sankt Hans
Hospital, Jan. 26, 19———") and by the undisguised complaints
made about the conditions offered to patients at this psychiatric
institution ("Could we please have a little influence here. Have
paid state and municipality"). The second space belongs in the
world of the fable and is characterized by a complete reversal of
the prevailing conditions ("All over the world", "By N. N.", who
"Am the government in Berlin" or, indeed, "I Berlin"). The first
part of the letter has to do with complaints; things are not quite
what they ought to be. In the second part of the letter these

deplorable conditions are constantly being put right, the text declaring that its First Person has seized power and is now in a position to catch the "monsters" that made havoc in the first part. At the same time the patient has somewhat diminished the distance, evident in the first part of the letter, between the First Person of the enunciation ("we," first and foremost) and the patient's proper name ("N. N."). In the conditions of power and grandeur prevailing in the second part, the patient writes distinctly "I N. N." The "I" of the enunciation is absent, more or less, in the first part: "Must Lie In Bed during the day," "Must have an operation," and "Want to be married, work" should probably be read as "I must lie in bed during the day," "I must have an operation," and so on, just as it is possible to translate "Chamber pots required" from the passive into the active voice in the form of "I require chamber pots when. . . ." Similarly, the many possible disguises for this unmarked First-Person instance in the enunciation are expressly mentioned in the text: one can "buy a felt mask," and "long hair can be stuck on the frock." But the "I" emerges again in the second part of the letter, where there is power and control: "if you please." This is the language of power.

But the concluding remarks in the text deny these movements from a here where things are bad to a there where there is power. The letter ends: "Refuted in the police for cure" and is signed "The paupers." It is true that the letter loses its "I" during its account of the concrete circumstances being complained about, and also that it performs a series of repair maneuvers of a symbolic kind by inserting the vanished "I" as a substitute for the missing influence. Nevertheless, the conclusion of the letter does appear to take account of reality, as in this way the text as a whole retains its hold on the reality to be complained about and criticized. The text voices a *criticism of power*.

In Table 7.1 we conclude this summary of our view of reality in schizophrenia by formalizing our observations of the various fundamental positions of enunciation and discourse in the letter "To Emperor."

Table 7.1. Relations of discourse and enunciation in the letter "To Emperor"

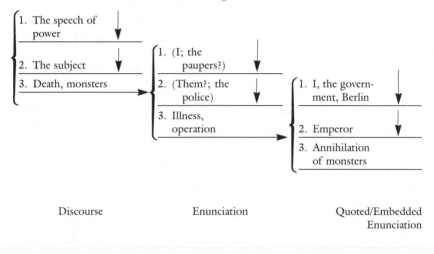

       Discourse   Enunciation   Quoted/Embedded
                                                    Enunciation

In Table 7.1 we see again how the instances in the enunciation have weak markings, while the discursive register breaks through into the embedded enunciation, which leads to performatives, that is, linguistic repairments. We also note that the structure of the body proper and of the body of the other is centered thematically around images of death and destruction on the one hand and of power and perpetuity on the other.

We have indicated that power and knowledge play an important part in the representation of reality in schizophrenia. The letter "To Emperor" is a clear example of the dual way in which many schizophrenics represent their relation to power and knowledge: As far as the First Person in the enunciation is concerned, there is a lack of power and knowledge (incompetence and ignorance); around the quoted or embedded utterances power and knowledge are restored, often by means of a claim that the speech or text was produced by some big name, a well-known person, and by the subject matter having to do with secrets of a high political order. In embedded utterances it is, indeed, the speech of the Other that is quoted without restraint, or the Other who is spoken to—the "Emperor," for instance.

It is difficult to analyze these relations of power and knowledge. The basis for their recurring function in schizophrenic speech should probably be sought in childhood. However, the ways these persons are treated by their family, school, workplace, and by welfare and health authorities also exert a great influence on their conception of power and knowledge.

In the mental structure of the schizophrenic, the main interest attaches to the marking of the body of the other. The body of the other is the place where the child carries out its identification with other human beings (frequently the mother). The various communicative relationships that the child takes part in, presumably very early, leave a special trace on the body of the other. Later in life the multitude of social relationships that the individual is part of constitute an impenetrable network of conscious and unconscious power relationships. Relations in the family; platonic or sexual relationships with sweethearts, friends, fellow students, and colleagues; relations at the place of work—all are deeply embedded in the relations of power that not only are present in speech but that also govern it. The effect that these relations of power have on the imaginary body threatened by schizophrenia is that, in the company of others, in the microuniverse of communication itself, the body will resist linguistically recognizable symbolic markings being imprinted or, rather, forced upon it. The problem now facing the person threatened by schizophrenia is that the body of the other does not function as the space of fantasmatic identification where the subject can be structured. As a result, the symbolic traces are not organized properly; instead, the body of the other becomes a mirror construction that is alienated, that is, located outside the individual's control and that more or less systematically distorts the modes of address in the speech, the speaker's particular representation of himself and his relationship to the world about him. Understood in this way, the body of the other becomes an asubjective but nevertheless personified element of the speech.

The structure of the body proper and the body of the other is everywhere subject to the laws laid down by the relationship between the Other and the other. It is imporant to hold on to the fact that the other, the receiver in the enunciation, also lays down definite laws and rules for, and sets limits to, the dialogue, since it is exactly the presence of the other that makes the processes of identification difficult. Merely to ask someone to speak, or to speak himself, can pose difficulties for the schizophrenic. A letter from a schizophrenic patient very clearly describes these give-and-take problems:

> Dear *Doctor* Smith
> Oh, one *consented* to *be silent* have. Wish one went *be silent. Leave it* be. *Let* me *have* that I am *lucky.* Wish one is *silent-lucky. Let* me *have* that *it* is *luck* that *it* is *silence* that is *asked* for; oh, *be silent* is *luck, wish* that is *luck.* But have *luck* with silence *without that* on *paper.* Wish one is *lucky* with *it.* [etc.]

However, many schizophrenics can easily administer the rules governing dialogues. For them it is not the more transient power relationships of the dialogue that cause problems—the parties in turn speaking and asking each other to speak; breaking into, correcting, or commenting on each other's speech; and the like. Rather, these are caused by the institutional exercise of power—inherent in differences of social position, education, class, and economic and political status. In everyday life it is a well-known fact that a high status within an institution, a hierarchy, a social system, or the like gives a speaker greatly improved possibilities of manipulating other people in conversations, debates, negotiations, and quarrels. The higher status automatically carries with it the right to speak out of turn, to break off negotiations, and in general to retain power in the space of speech. But it is precisely those features which imply conversational power that cause the schizophrenic to react so vehemently. In the cracks or openings in the conversation where real power manifests itself—for example, in the distribution of speech—we may observe the schizophrenic withdrawing completely from the necessary process in which the speakers speak or ask others to speak, express themselves or are silent, without regard to any chairman. It is in cases like this that the schizophrenic person may fail entirely to include in his speech its receiver, the Second Person of the enunciation. To the schizophrenic, the other then no longer exists as a separate and in principle ignorant instance that must be "talked into" accepting the validity of what is being said. In the schizophrenic, the dialectic putting oneself in the other's place is hampered by the fact that the body of the other as the place where identification takes place is rejected and fragmented.

From this account one might get the impression that the body of the other has some kind of independent existence. That is not the case. We have described the difficulties of identification in the conversational exercise of power as centered around the body of the other. From a theoretical point of view the body of the other is the place where these difficulties are located. But we ought everywhere to have involved the body proper as a complementary entity of the body of the other. The body proper is the place to which desire and aggressivity can be assigned (or ascribed): it is only a body insofar as it constitutes the reverse of the extroversion of the body of the other.

The body of the other is in a way the outside of the body, and the body proper is the body's inwardness representing the essence of aggressivity, namely death. When the body of the other breaks down, when it springs a leak, it is the destructiveness of the body proper that spills out.

It is important to note that this distribution of thematic values and qualities around the body proper and body of the other is socially determined: it is specifically constituted from one society to another, from one mode of production to another, and most certainly from one class to another (the exploited class relates to the body—and to its being worn down or destroyed—in a different way from the exploiting class).[3] But regardless of the values thematically assigned to the poles of the structure of the body proper and the body of the other, it is the body proper that spaces, separates, and articulates the fantasms that together make up the imaginary body. The lack of repression in schizophrenia should be understood as an effect of the body proper in the subject—an effect that is constantly repeating its interference with the formations of the body of the other. The schizophrenic *experiences* this as an effect of the destructiveness of the body proper manifesting itself explicitly in the position of the First Person in the enunciation. We saw this in the letter "To Emperor," where the masked "I" wrote that she had got a "felt mask" and "you only feel a splash in the deep water"; and it is precisely "Living people who want monster",—the "I" of the speech that is the element most frequently subjected to the characteristic workings of the body proper, whereas the body of the other just as frequently finds its place in the embedded enunciations that provide the script for the fable. The fantasmatic foundation of the imaginary body has been "undermined," as one patient said. Its signifiers, originating from the register of discourse, dominate both the enunciation and the registers of the embedded enunciations (see the tabulation of the letter "To Emperor" in Table 7.1). In other words, the imagination is allowed free rein, as we say, although it is in many respects a rein that is extremely unfree, especially in regard to the appearance of the elements, the signifiers, in the different registers of speech.

But the effect of the body proper on the registers of enunciation—for instance, in the form of a disguise resembling death or eternity—lead not only to diffuse or weakly marked, masked, or evacuated First-Person instances but also to a sometimes all-pervasive breakthrough or migration of signifiers from widely different discursive contexts into the registers of enunciation. Here these signifiers will lodge anywhere and always with a great variety of Second-Person anchoring points. See our analysis of the sentence "Yes, yes, and I wrote his discharge for Nazareth in Austria yesterday with my pencil".

There is, therefore, in the schizophrenic reaction to relations of power not only an express *criticism of power* but also an attempted *exercise of power* of a symbolic nature.

Power and knowledge are not in themselves evils, neither objectively nor as viewed from the patient's understanding of his or her environment. The situation is that the power and knowledge relationships between patient and therapist can be used by both the patient and the therapist to establish the necessary provisional but gradually more stable *transference* that forms the basis of the incipient investigation by both parties of the positions in the parties' speech where recognition occurs; where, in other words, it becomes possible to make the positions of the speech objective so that the patient's splitting can be referred to the position in his or her own speech.

In the reality of schizophrenia this is an extremely difficult process. On the one hand, an institutional speech prevails in which the patient both *is* an entry in a book and *feels* that way; on the other hand, the therapist may represent the reality that the patient wants to take part in and become a respected member of. This ambivalent duality in the subject structure of the patient corresponds at certain points to the therapist's own ambivalence: on the one hand, the patient represents a good object, since the therapist makes a living out of giving help and believes that he is capable of doing so. On the other hand, the patient represents an evil object insofar as the therapist is confronted with anxiety and fear. In the concluding chapter we shall therefore describe the therapeutic functions of the therapist's speech and ideas.

CHAPTER EIGHT

TREATMENT WITH SCHIZOPHRENICS

COUNTERTRANSFERENCE: THE POSITION OF THE THERAPIST

Many books in the field of psychiatry express the view that the ability of schizophrenics to communicate rationally and purposefully has been seriously damaged. According to this view, the possibility of conversing meaningfully with the schizophrenic and of achieving mutual empathy is severely curtailed. Moreover, according to many psychological and psychiatric theories, it is characteristic of the thinking of schizophrenics to be concrete, vague, and unstructured, rather than abstract and logically developed. Such theories are actually based on an interpretation of schizophrenic language. Since schizophrenic *texts* appear deficient, schizophrenic thinking is believed to be defective. These theories, then, take as their point of departure a belief in a normal language that expresses normal thinking of an abstract and logically developed kind.

There is no reason to enter into a discussion here of these many theories, as all are content with simply identifying a cognitive or emotional communication defect in the schizophrenic person. In our view, this is a misleading hypothesis.

Our description of schizophrenics' linguistic capacity has sometimes led us to talk about a failure of deixis or a damaged imaginary body, but this in no way implies that schizophrenics are defective or deficient either emotionally or linguistically. In schizophrenia there is a breakthrough of discursive elements without enunciative orientation, often with an intense experience of anxiety, linked not only to the signifiers but also to the fundamental pattern of organization in which fantasy operates.

In many conversations with schizophrenics, the utterances, arguments, fables, and the like produced by the schizophrenic serve to expose a life that has often been extremely difficult. Of course, the dynamics of the intersubjective processes can be such that conversation can be carried out only with the greatest difficulty. A therapist is often faced with unpredictable interruptions in the process of therapy, such as unexpected, vehement, and unaccountable outbursts of aggression. At other times the interruption can be very quiet, and one has the feeling of being neglected: one disappears as the Second Person to whom the patient speaks, in spite of the patient's physical presence in the space of reality. Sometimes the patient will continue to speak more or less in monologue. To the therapist the sentences then appear as chains of expressions whose meaning is not readily understandable but whose significance the patient evidently regards as simple and obvious.

Often the therapist will respond to the patient's anxiety and aggressive behavior with corresponding and simultaneous chains of ideas, fantasies, and emotions. This often happens in cases where the therapist begins therapy with the hope he will maintain a secure position in the face of the unexpected situations that are dominated by the breakthrough of metonymies and the displacement of the instances of enunciations. With other patients, or in other situations, the therapist may experience an autistic contact from the patient that reflects and provokes various forms of withdrawal maneuvers on the part of the therapist. Confusion, unproductive silences, inadequate ideas, or a formal or routine attitude to the patient—these are not uncommon reactions in therapists in such situations. As Searles says:

> I have learned the hard way, by contrast, that any chronically schizophrenic patient is in, at the beginning of our work, at least as strong a

position as my own. There are certain processes in him which (working in conjunction with the mores of our medical profession) render him enormously formidable, interpersonally, to any analyst who presumes to help him, and the fact that these processes are not predominantly within the patient's conscious control seems often to strengthen, rather than weaken, the patient's power position as perceived by the analyst. The latter inevitably becomes deeply embroiled, at a conscious level, in conflictual feeling including intense guilt and self-condemnation, feelings not merely of his "own" but, often more predominantly, feelings being projected into him by the patient who remains successfully defended, at an unconscious level, against experiencing these in awareness.[1]

Depending on the transference relationship and the therapeutic setting, the therapist may react in many different ways. If the patient, for example, complains of impudent "addressing persons in a wireless way" and "telephone shots in the head and the nose," the therapist can:

1. Defend himself by not responding; or by saying that the opinion proposed is nonsense and that he, the therapist, does not understand him, so could he please express himself in another way;
2. Tell the patient that he, the therapist, does not know where the meaning of the utterances is leading to, so maybe they can further explore the content together;
3. Tell the patient that such thoughts also cause anxiety and disquiet in the therapist; or
4. Ask the patient who the "addressing persons" might be or in what way the "telephone shots in the head and the nose" relate to the therapist.

These four different ways of reacting are of course only examples; it is easy to imagine a variety of reactions that fall outside the framework of these examples, or reactions that consist of several different ways of relating to the utterance at one and the same time.

To the extent that a totally autistic or defenselessly receptive patient gives no outward indication of any form of reality that the therapist's words can capture or be adjusted to, the patient in a way deprives the therapist of his authority and power in the conversation. The patient is superior insofar as it is only the therapist who seems to have any wish for contact. But to lose the feeling of autonomy in situations like this, where the therapist is institutionally charged with embodying authority and representing reality, has a considerable effect on the therapist's subject structure. This effect can express, manifest, and consolidate itself in a variety of ways. The consolidation is an effect of the countertransference. Underlying the countertransference is the fact that the therapist's response is an echo of a body of texts in which the therapist's own prejudices, qualifications, knowledge, and complexes of emotions circulate in the register of discourse.[2]

The effect of countertransference is a series of phenomena that are unmistakably present in any dialogue in psychiatric institutions. The staff will see daily examples, even in the most trivial episodes, of the interference of countertransference. Whether he wants to or not, the therapist will be involved in the dynamics of intersubjective processes; the interfering processes repeat themselves again and again in the spaces in which the therapeutic contact takes place. Viewed from this angle, getting to know the patient's peculiarities consists in establishing a pattern for the effects of countertransference, as a result of which the contact with the patient becomes one of familiarity and routine.

If the countertransference is not dealt with theoretically and practically, it is difficult to avoid a contact, and consequently a form of treatment, that are governed to a decisive degree by what we might call *the discourse of the institution*: attitudes and prejudices dictated by the walls, territories, and traditions of the psychiatric institution, the results of a long sequence of historically based ideological, political, economic and cultural circumstances. This is not only a question of the institution's politically and economically determined prescriptions for staff, the politically and ideologically functioning hierarchies of power and knowledge, the type and extent of the therapy offered to patients, and the training and supervision offered to staff. It is also a question of the physical environment in which the institution operates.

All these factors may contribute to a situation in which the countertransference is experienced less as interference than as the established mode of behavior of the institution. Therefore, the patient's reactions to this interference are generally sanctioned by the institution. The interference of countertransference seems by and large to be obscured by, and absorbed into, the view of normality that prevails in the institution: the patient's speech is perceived as the exercise of a relatively well defined pathological form of contact, the processes of which are located outside the therapist's area of control. In contrast, the therapist's speech is perceived as transmitting a realistic, sensible, and corrective communication, the processes of which are located within the therapist's area of control. The therapist controls his speech and knows what it means. Thus, the therapist confronts the patient as the incarnation of power and knowledge.

In the everyday practice of institutional psychiatry there has been scant criticism of, and little practical work done on, countertransference. The lack of criticism and thorough work in this area is one reason why institutions continue to maintain a type of discourse that is saturated with the diagnostics of medical terminology.

THE THERAPIST'S POSITION IN THE PATIENT'S SPEECH

In this chapter we shall try to illustrate the relationship between patient and therapist, that is to say, between a subject structure that generates hallucinatory fantasmatic ideas on the one hand and the subject of the therapist who is caught up in this universe of fantasies on the other hand. We shall also discuss the basis of the assumption that the therapist always constitutes an element—as a transference figure—in the patient's production of fantasies.

We assume that any speech—including any form of thinking or

interior monologue—takes place via a continuous production of fantasms, an exercise of fantasy, which is in part individual and in part social: we might call it a socially determined subjective production of fantasms. Thus, actual fact and reality are not, as is commonly supposed, categories in sharp contrast to the concept of fantasy. A very large number of socially existing ideological images, figures, and ideas are in the nature of fantasies and forms part of, for example, the entertainment programs of the mass media. It makes no sense to present the relationship between reality and fantasy exclusively as one of a number of alternatives. For therapeutic purposes, consequently, it is also not in itself productive to deal with the question of reality or fantasy as one of a number of alternatives. What goes on in therapy is complicated because—prior to either the patient or the therapist acquiring any knowledge or consciousness of it—the therapist's subject structure may already have been implanted as an actively working element in the registers of the patient's speech. On the other hand, this may give the therapist extensive possibilities—also in relation to the delusions in the patient's representation of reality—for exploring the position that the therapist occupies and the values by which he is judged by the patient: the therapist may be in a position of giving or taking, may be knowing or ignorant, positively or negatively defined, powerful or powerless. It is the exploration of these values and positions that is decisive for whether it will be possible to re-form the patient's subject structure in the course of the therapy.

The question is where the therapist as a subject structure is placed in the registers of the patient's speech. In what ways is it possible to attract the patient's transferences to oneself? In what way is it possible to work on one's own subject structure so that the patient gets the possibility of tracking down her or his own position there?

All these questions seem urgent and exacting ones, not only in prolonged courses of therapy, but also in the little conversations about trivial things in everyday life. An elderly paranoid schizophrenic patient would, for example, accept and trust only those members of the staff who had been incorporated into her world of fantasies—a world in which she herself was queen and the others in the ward were various personages of different rank and worth in the gallery of characters surrounding her highness. Another patient with the same diagnosis might converse for hours about events she had learned about from the ward's television and radio, magazines and newspapers. It was possible to talk with her about West German terrorists, about different zoological topics, and about the negotiations between the Danish Underground Consortium and the government about oil leases. There was nothing remarkable in all this, apart from the fact that during the conversation she insisted on sitting with pursed lips and with one hand under her anus because her speech made it possible for "animal spirits" from the ground to penetrate the orifices of her body and destroy her internal organs ("undermine" her, to use her own expression). She preferred not to speak of this to the uninitiated. If she was pressed to give a more detailed description of these things, she would often give a short answer: people would just think she was mad, she might reply. If she was nevertheless persuaded to elaborate, she would, in telling her story, very strongly emphasize that what she was speaking about was reality, a reality whose existence was beyond any doubt whatsoever.

If others disagreed with her, it was just because they had yet to realize what she had recognized as true. Her belief that her own words were anchored to reality was unshakable and indisputable—exactly the same unshakability that often characterized people's belief in the truth of social ideologies, or widespread beliefs whose content is reinforced by the fact that a large group of people regard them as self-evident, absolutely valid, and historically true.

The effect on the patient of the fact that her fable about the animal spirits undermining her would be hard for other people to understand was that she failed to include her conversation partner in her speech. Rarely did she attach any importance to the understanding of her conversation partner of the universe she was describing. Rather, she would relate her fable without paying any regard to the presence of the other. Often her manner would be forced and institutionalized, sometimes stereotyped and mechanical. In such situations, the entire enunciation characterizing the relationship between patient and therapist was governed by signifiers of the register of discourse. Accordingly, the patient's speech was dominated by metonymic relations between signifiers destroying or annihilating the signified.

The patient's speech, however, was not unstructured. It was organized in accordance with the syntax that structures the signifiers of the imaginary body, more precisely the relation between the imaginary body and the patient's experience of herself and her surroundings. The imaginary body was constantly threatened by a collapse of meaning, that is, of the signified. Elements of the fragmented body were projected and appeared as an outward threat. As to the syntax of the imaginary body, it consisted on the one hand in idealized positions, places where "the celestial animal spirits are" and where "they have organized themselves in the place where their needs can be fulfilled"; on the other hand, dangerous positions were thematized as a place for "the troublesome underground animal spirits" that "have nothing and are lying any which way in layers." It was because they possessed nothing that they were motivated to come out and destroy the patient's internal organs, as mentioned earlier.

After many hours of therapy, the transference to the therapist was sufficiently powerful to enable him to establish himself in a position where the patient's speech was tied to the therapist. The therapist was now integrated in the patient's subject structure and was able to acquire a positive value in such a way that he became a relatively stable element in the patient's speech.

Needless to say, the patient continued to thematize her sufferings, constantly repeating her attempts to come to grips with her experiences textually, and continuing to take precautions against those events in the world that were brought on by the fantasms. But her narratives changed character; her tales acquired a new style. There was now in her representation a recurring concern that the therapist might also be subjected to the hardships that she was herself a victim of and under which she suffered. She expressed anxiety, uncertainty, and insecurity with regard to the therapist's fate. Moreover, it was now possible for the therapist to make the patient connect her fantasmatic ideas in a much more stable way with a string of associations concerning actual events in her life. Thus, the therapist—after having installed himself as the Second Person in the patient's speech—was able gradually to bring the patient's ideas into contact with the reality to which speech had lost its anchorings. In this phase of the treatment the patient started to think that some of her ideas probably derived from the strongly religious upbringing she had been given by her father.

This change in the relationship between the patient and the therapist might seem very small indeed, especially since the delusions, the tales of fantasy, neither disappeared nor significantly diminished. But, from the point of view of psychotherapy, it was a decisive change because it was a change in the patient's possibilities of symbolizing her subject structure. The changed possibilities of symbolization meant that the patient was able to occupy new positions in relation to the fantasms that continued to circulate in the registers of her speech. Where the patient before had had to repeat her fables again and again in a stereotyped manner without regard to the understanding of any other person, it was now possible for at least one other person—the therapist—to alter the patient's relationship to her ideas, at least in part. But what did this change consist in? How can it be described from the point of view of the patient's subject structure? In the following section we shall describe the two phases of treatment which were marked out by the change.

TWO PHASES OF TREATMENT

In the first phase of the treatment, the patient was rather autistic vis-à-vis the therapist. In therapy, the space where formal contact took place between patient and therapist was separated from the space in which the patient had to tell about her different kinds of unpleasant experiences. In the first phase, the enunciative relations were made indistinct and often incomprehensible to outsiders, including the therapist. The patient's speech was dominated by the oppositions fixed by the imaginary body's syntax: a positively marked position characterized by the patient regarding her self as being pleasurably protected by the body of the other, and a negatively marked position characterized by the patient experiencing her body as being disintegrated, divided between the fantasms of the body proper and the body of the other.

The patient's imaginary speech was not directed to anyone in particular in her surroundings. But the speech swung strongly between two extreme points. She employed two radically different styles when talking, which seemed striking and unforeseeable to everyone on the staff. One style was characterized by hallucinatory and transitivistic notions of the influence of the many "animal spirits." The patient spoke as if she had no feelings and no pain.

The other style was characterized by autism in that the patient either made total retreats or allowed her account to be subject to the stereotyped automatic mechanisms that the fable could provoke. Together the two positions constituted a fundamental ambivalence. The one position never existed without the other. The positive and negative poles of this ambivalence could not reach a compromise and were inextricably joined in a mirrorlike mutual relationship.

Thus, in this first phase the patient could talk to anyone—any Tom, Dick, or Harry—as in the last instance the speech was addressed only to the Other. The therapist's role as conversation partner was completely unimportant. The patient's account lacked any Second-Person anchorings. No fully valid listener existed for the patient at this stage. At the same time, her tone of voice, receptivity, humor, awareness, and interest in her own condition varied a lot.

The second phase of the therapy was no longer dominated by

the patient's "non-existence" in relation to the therapist. In this phase the patient succeeded in placing her subject in an imaginary relationship to the therapist in such a way that it was possible for her to bring the syntax of the fragmented imaginary body into a kind of stable, textual symbolic position, where the constant appearance of the fantasies gradually allowed themselves to be attached to reality.

In the therapeutic relation this reality was naturally attached to the therapist's speech. The stable position gained or occupied by the imaginary body in the second phase of the therapy was characterized by a kind of giving of gifts. The patient's speech—both in its noncontrollable form, where it incessantly alternated between the two styles, and in its more trivial form, where it was a matter of everyday events such as meals—was directly or indirectly given to the other in the enunciation, that is, primarily given to the therapist.

In contrast to the more or less globally marked fantasms in the patient's speech, the space of speech was gradually adapted to the concrete and locally present person in the space of speech: the patient built up a stable Second Person in her speech. Even though the conversation with the patient could still be marked by delusions and body fables, or more generally by the patient's lack of respect or consideration for the persons, time, space, and relations of social reality, the therapist was clearly and expressly a part of the patient's presentation, not just in the indications of speech, but also in eye-contact indications of the presence of the Second Person in the speaker's text. The imaginary world in which the patient lived and suffered was replaced by a more symbolically marked perception of being together with the therapist. And the whole imaginary universe that the patient experienced gradually began to lose the absolute truth value that the patient previously had attributed to it in her presentation of reality.

In the first phase of the treatment, she was unable to represent the body of the other to the other she was talking to. Therefore, she could not *present* her body of the other (see Chapter 6). The repression of the body proper–body of the other structure in her speech never functioned; on the contrary, she experienced or perceived her self as an element whom anyone could see was persecuted by "bothersome animal spirits." She therefore had to protect her bodily orifices against any vile "undermining." Her body of the other tended to melt in with every external object, including every other person. The body of the other was at worst a threat in the external world, a danger to the patient's life and welfare. And in this connection the registers of speech were perforated and broken down.

But when the therapist in the second phase was able to unite some elements of the fable *and* his own position, the patient was equally able to comment on her own speech. In this way the reestablishment of the division between the different deictically given spaces was begun. The space of speech was now no longer dominated by the delusional "animal spirits," and the patient's perception of her body no longer constantly broke into the dialogue in unpredictable and threatening ways. The patient's whole subject structure was in the process of being dominated by the symbolic giving of the imaginary figures that the patient was unaware of and that achieved meaning only when they were answered by the therapist.

On the level of enunciation, this meant that patient and the therapist could share something, namely the series of fantasms that the patient's fable, precisely in this second phase, would gradually construct and sometimes comment on and explain. At the same time, in this second phase of the treatment it could be observed that the patient showed concern for the therapist, first and foremost insofar as he was identified with the patient's own person by being included in her fable. In psychiatric textbooks this identification is usually regarded as a symptom of deterioration. As a link between the first and second phases of the treatment, however, identification must be regarded as an important step in reestablishing viable tranference relations between therapist and patient.

As this example shows, it is of decisive importance that the patient has the opportunity to distance himself or herself from his or her notions and thus perhaps to participate actively in objectifying them. As Freud wrote, "The patient's comments on her unintelligible remark have the value of an analysis."[3]

The patient's spontaneous analysis is not essentially different from the therapist's analysis and intervention in the transition from the first phase to the second. It is the process of making the notions symbolic that is decisive.

A therapist in the psychiatric institution, with its institutional rhythm and its special forms of treatment and social intercourse, all too often realizes that schizophrenic patients do not get the opportunity to carry out this necessary work with their frequently painful fantasms. Patients whom the institution regards as chronic are people whose fantasms have set in an untreated position. The patients' immediate surroundings, the conditions of their everyday lives are marked by other people becoming accustomed to their fantasmatic notions. In other words, it is rather the patient's surroundings than the patient herself that have objectified the structure and content of her schizophrenic speech.

Whether the patients are chronic or are people with severe or less severe psychotic conditions, they need competent psychotherapeutic treatment. Under other social conditions where demands as to working capacity and judgment were different and where concepts like social disablement did not deprive people of their rationality and civil rights, it might rather have been a case of a need for "guidance" or perhaps "political reeducation."

"IT'S A TAPE THAT'S SPEAKING"

Schizophrenics experience their thoughts and speech as being constrained or "recorded" to a greater or lesser degree. All speech and thought is more or less constrained. But in contrast to the speech of socially and mentally well functioning people, schizophrenic speech is subject to the processes caused by the fragmentation of the imaginary body. These processes are not essentially changed by the speech of the institution, which seems just as constrained as schizophrenic talk. Effective psychotherapeutic treatment of schizophrenics can take place only when psychodynamic and textually competent relationships have been established.

Therefore, it is necessary to analyze the reality that schizophrenic speech expresses. It is impossible to understand and treat schizophrenia without including the absolutely central relationship between the other and the Other, without including the basic ignorance shared by patient and therapist at the beginning of the therapy, or without analyzing the diverse fantasms and the expressions of the imaginary body. Without detailed knowledge of the positions of speech, any psychotherapeutic analysis will be powerless.

NOTES

INTRODUCTION

1. Each year the Institute of Psychiatric Demography (in Aarhus, Denmark) contributes material on this subject to the *Danish Medical Report* (report on hospitals and other institutions for the treatment of sick in Denmark; Sundhedsstyrelsen, Copenhagen). There is, moreover, a fairly recent comprehensive survey in Betaenkning no. 826 from the Danish Ministry of the Interior (1977).

2. The total institution concept is in common use in literature on sociology; it is discussed extensively in Goffman (1961) and (1968).

3. An inquiry by questionnaire, which was carried out in 1977 (Rosenberg & Reisby [1978]), showed that more than 85% of the research being done in Denmark today in adult psychiatry is biologically oriented. The remaining 15% is made up chiefly of social psychiatry, which is dominated in Denmark by genetic-epidemiological research. Although the figures of the inquiry should be taken with some reservations, and although psychiatric research is also done by nonmedical institutions (the Institute for Social Research, institutes for psychological and sociological studies, etc.), the predominance of the biological approach in contemporary psychiatric research seems to be an established fact.

4. Bleuler made this statement in a critical and often-overlooked essay, *Das Autistisch-Undisziplinierte Denken in der Medizin und seine Überwindung* (1919) (*Autistic Undisciplined Thinking in Medicine and How to Overcome it* [1970]).

5. Lacan (1966), pp. 531–583; English translation, Lacan (1977), pp. 179–225.

6. Many scientific works lend support to this assumption; see Dunham (1976).

CHAPTER ONE

1. These are excerpts from an interview we made in 1976. It is included here with the permission of the patient and her closest relatives. As is the case with all the letters and the other texts we make use of in this book, we have in this interview deleted anything that might contribute to an identification of the patient. If names of living or deceased persons occur in the text, they have likewise been deleted or replaced by initials or by N. N. (in the case of letter writers). Indications of time (dates) and place (e.g., addresses) have been deleted or altered. Here and throughout, "I" and "P" mean interviewer and patient, respectively.

2. The letters were written by a now deceased female patient.

CHAPTER TWO

1. The letter was written by a now deceased male patient.

2. Thematic analysis is sometimes also called thematological analysis. It is, first and foremost, the analysis of content. See Greimas (1966).

3. Narrative (or narratological) analysis is discussed in detail in Bremond (1973).

4. The French journal *Langages* has published a special issue on enunciation analysis (no. 17, 1970).

5. The concept of discourse, as used here, largely corresponds to the concept described in Foucault (1969) (English translation [1972]), but it does *not* correspond to the concept of discourse as it is used in British and American linguistics.

6. These quotations are from an article entitled "La métaphore du sujet" ("The Metaphor of the Subject") in Lacan (1966), pp. 889–892.

7. The example corresponds to the discussion in Fillmore (1966). See also Fillmore (1971).

8. The examples are parallel to the ones used in Wunderlich (1971).

9. Fillmore (1971).

10. Freud (1900), *Standard Edition* (1953), Vols. 4–5.

11. Saussure (1972); English translation (1974).

12. Freud (1938), *Standard Edition* (1964), Vol. 23, p. 175.

13. Greenson (1967), p. 155.

14. Freud (1923), *Standard Edition* (1966), Vol. 19, p. 34.

15. Lacan (1966), English translation (1977), p. 193.

16. The concept of the Other corresponds to Lacan's concept of *l'Autre*, the other with a capital O.

CHAPTER THREE

1. This is the same patient who was interviewed in Chapter 1.

2. Freud (1915a), *Standard Edition* (1957), Vol. 14, p. 136.

3. See also Laplanche & Pontalis (1973), pp. 382–385.

4. In *Die endliche und unendliche Analyse*, Freud (1937) (*Analysis Terminable and Interminable*), *Standard Edition*, (1964), Vol. 23, pp. 216–253.

5. The letter was written by a now deceased female patient.

6. Bartolucci & Albers (1974), p. 131.

7. The letter was written by a male patient.

8. In a footnote to the article *Das Unbewusste* (Freud 1915b) (*The Unconscious*), *Standard Edition*, Vol. 14, pp. 159–215.

CHAPTER FOUR

1. This concept was originally presented by Eugen Bleuler (1911), who characterized autism as a certain *Loslösung von der Wirklichkeit* (detachment from reality) and a *Zurückgezogenheit auf sich selbst* (withdrawal into oneself). To Bleuler, the concept of autism is far more differentiated than many contemporary textbooks on psychiatry would lead one to believe. Thus, he makes these

distinctions: "autistic world," "autistic feeling," "autistic thoughts," and "autistic thinking." See also Bleuler (1919).

2. *Transitivismus* (transitivism) is a term which occurs very early in psychiatry, in Bleuler (1911) among others. Transitivism is the phenomenon that a patient transfers parts of his or her thoughts or personality to another person; this "otherness" then comes to control the patient in various ways.

3. The term "influencing machine" has been taken from an admirably precise and weighty article by Victor Tausk (1919). In it, Tausk attempts to describe the syntax that contributes to the construction of the imagined "influencing machine" in the patient and gives an account of the patient's phase-by-phase construction of the fantasy that shapes his identity.

4. This psychoanalytical term is discussed in Laplanche & Pontalis (1973), pp. 292–293.

5. In his two short articles from 1924, *Neurose und Psychose* (*Neurosis and Psychosis*) and *Der Realitätsverlust bei Neurose und Psychose* (*The Loss of Reality in Neurosis and Psychosis*), Freud describes the hallucinations and delusions of psychosis as substitute formations for the "lost" reality. Both articles: *Standard Edition* (1961), Vol. 19, pp. 149–153 and pp. 183–187.

CHAPTER FIVE

1. We are here thinking of a long tradition that builds on works by Head (1920), Schilder (1923), and others.

2. See Lacan (1977), pp. 1–7 and 8–29.

3. The relationship between body and "truth" was analyzed by (among others) Bataille (1957) and Foucault (1969, 1976).

4. See, e.g., Mette (1928), Navratil (1966), and Arieti (1967).

5. Lacan (1977), p. 153.

6. Smith (1946), p. 155.

7. See Freud's definition of the hallucinations and delusions of psychosis as substitute formations for the "lost" reality: Freud (1924b), *Standard Edition* (1961), Vol. 19, p. 187.

8. "Language is language, and there is only one sort of language: concrete language . . . that people talk," says Lacan (1970), p. 180.

9. Lemaire (1977), p. 142.

CHAPTER SIX

1. A summary of some classical viewpoints is given in Laplanche & Pontalis (1973), pp. 78–80.

2. Lacan (1977), p. 2.

3. Lacan (1977), p. 19.

4. Lemaire (1977), pp. 78–92; here a pedagogical account is given of the relations among language acquisition, repression, and the Oedipus complex.

5. In accordance with Derrida (1966) (English translation 1977), we understand by *spacing* the principles for the articulation of the signifier that are observed in writing: the combination and separation of letters in the articulation of meaning.

6. Lacan (1977), p. 11.
7. Laplanche (1976), Chapter 5, and Laplanche & Pontalis (1973).
8. Freud (1915a), *Standard Edition* (1957), Vol. 14, p. 136.
9. See Laplanche & Pontalis (1973), pp. 349–356.
10. Freud (1911), *Standard Edition* (1958), Vol. 12, p. 63.
11. See Segal (1975).
12. See the article "The Signification of the Phallus" in Lacan (1977), pp. 281–291.
13. In Lacan (1977), pp. 179–225, there is a summary of a reading of "the Schreber Case" and, along with it, an account of some basic mechanisms in the pathology of psychosis. A reader's guide is given by John P. Muller and William Richardson (1982).
14. Laplanche & Pontalis (1973), p. 166.

CHAPTER SEVEN

1. The interviewee is a now deceased female patient.
2. The letter was written by a now deceased female patient. It was written during World War II, and the particular, dated significance of elements like "Berlin," "America," "decadences," and statements like "Germany is Danish" should not be overlooked.
3. Studies in comparative psychiatry—within the field called ethnopsychiatry among others—have shown obvious differences in the area of body proper-–body of the other; see Wulff (1972), in particular *Psychiatrischer Bericht aus Vietnam* ("Psychiatric Report from Vietnam"), pp. 15–94.

CHAPTER EIGHT

1. Searles (1976), p. 585.
2. See also Laplanche & Pontalis (1973), pp. 92–93.
3. Freud (1915b), *Standard Edition* (1957), Vol. 14, p. 199.

REFERENCES

Arieti, S. (1967): *The Intrapsychic Self: Feeling, Cognition and Creativity in Health and Mental Illness.* New York: Basic Books.

Bartolucci, G. & R. J. Albers (1974): "Deictic Categories in the Language of Autistic Children." *Journal of Autism and Childhood Schizophrenia* 4: 131–141.

Bataille, G. (1957): *L'érotisme.* Paris: Minuit.

Betaenkning fra psykiatriudvalget (1977): *Den psykiatriske sygehusfunktion.* Betaenkning no. 826. Copenhagen.

Bleuler, E. (1911): *Dementia Praecox oder der Gruppe die Schizophrenien.* Leipzig: Deuticke. English translation, *Dementia Praecox or the Group of Schizophrenia.* New York 1950: International Universities Press.

——— (1919): *Autistic Undisciplined Thinking in Medicine and How to Overcome It.* Translated and edited by E. Harms, with a preface by Manfred Bleuler. Connecticut 1970: Hafner Publishing Co.

Bremond, C. (1973): *La logique du récit.* Paris: Editions du Seuil.

Derrida, J. (1966): *Freud et la scène de l'écriture. Critique* no. 230, Paris. English translation: *Freud and the Scene of Writing. Yale French Studies* (1977), no. 55–56: 74–117.

Dunham, H. W. (1976): *Society, Culture and Mental Disorder. Archives of General Psychiatry,* Vol. 33: 147–157.

Fillmore, C. (1966): *Deictic Categories in the Semantics of "Come." Word,* no. 19: 208–231.

——— (1971): *Santa Cruz Lectures On Deixis.* Berkeley 1975: University of California.

Foucault, M. (1969): *L'archéologie du savoir.* Paris: Gallimard. English translation, *The Archeology of Knowledge.* London 1972: Tavistock.

——— (1976): *La volonté du savoir.* Paris: Gallimard. English translation, *The History of Sexuality.* London 1979: Allen Lane.

Freud, S. (1900): *Die Traumdeutung.* Eng. *The Interpretation of Dreams. Standard Edition* (S.E.), Vol. 4–5. London 1953: Hogarth Press.

———— (1911): *Psychoanalytische Bemerkungen über einen auto-biographisch beschriebenen Fall von Paranoia (Dementia Para-noides)*. Eng. *Psycho-Analytic Notes on an Autobiographical Account of a Case of Paranoia (Dementia Paranoides)*. S.E., Vol. 12: 3–82. London 1958: Hogarth Press.

———— (1915a): *Triebe und Triebschicksale*. Eng. *Instincts and their Vicissitudes*. S.E., Vol. 14: 111–140. London 1957: Hogarth Press.

———— (1915b): *Das Unbewusste*. Eng. *The Unconscious*. S.E., Vol. 14: 159–215. London 1957: Hogarth Press.

———— (1923): *Das Ich und das Es*. Eng. *The Ego and the Id*. S.E., Vol. 19: 12–66. London 1966: Hogarth Press.

———— (1924a): *Neurose und Psychose*. Eng. *Neurosis and Psychosis*. S.E., Vol. 19: 149–153. London 1961: Hogarth Press.

———— (1924b): *Der Realitätsverlust bei Neurose und Psychose*. Eng. *The Loss of Reality in Neurosis and Psychosis*. S.E., Vol. 19: 183–187. London 1961: Hogarth Press.

———— (1937): *Die endliche und unendliche Analyse*. Eng. *Analysis Terminable and Interminable*. S.E., Vol. 23: 216–253. London 1964: Hogarth Press.

———— (1938): *Abriss der Psychoanalyse*. Eng. *An Outline of Psycho-Analysis*. S.E., Vol. 23: 144–207. London 1964: Hogarth Press.

Goffman, E. (1961): *On the Characteristics of Total Institution*. In: Cressey, D. R. (ed.): *The Prison*. New York: Holt, Rinehart and Winston.

———— (1968): *Asylums*. Harmondsworth: Penguin.

Greenson, R. R. (1967): *The Technique and Practice of Psycho-Analysis*. London: Hogarth Press.

Greimas, A. J. (1966): *Sémantique structurale*. Paris: Larousse.

Head, H. (1920): *Studies in Neurology*. Vol. 2. London.

Klein, M. (1946): *Notes on Some Schizoid Mechanisms*. In: *Envy and Gratitude and Other Works 1946–1963*. New York 1975: Delacorte Press/Seymour Laurence.

Lacan, J. (1966): *Écrits*. Paris: Editions du Seuil.

———— (1970): *Of Structure as an Inmixing of an Otherness Prerequisite to Any Subject Whatever*. In: Macksey, R. & E. Donato (eds.): *The Structuralist Controversy*. Baltimore & London: Johns Hopkins University Press.

———— (1977): *Écrits. A Selection*. London: Tavistock Publication.

Laplanche, J. (1976): *Life and Death in Psycho-Analysis*. Baltimore & London: Johns Hopkins University Press.

Laplanche, J. & J.-B. Pontalis (1973): *The Language of Psycho-Analysis*. London: Hogarth Press.

Lemaire, A. (1977): *Jacques Lacan*. London: Routledge and Kegan Paul.

Mette, A. (1928): *Über Beziehungen zwischen Spracheigentümlichkeiten schizophrener und dichterischer Produktion*. Dessau: Dion.

Muller, J. P. & W. J. Richardson (1982): *Lacan and Language*. New York: International Universities Press.

Navratil, L. (1966): *Schizophrenie und Sprache*. München: Deutscher Taschenbuch Verlag.

Rosenberg, R. & N. Reisby (1978): *Dansk voksenpsykiatrisk forskning* (Psychiatric Research in Denmark). *Ugeskrift for Laeger* no. 140: 551–556.

Saussure, F. de (1972): *Cours de linguistique générale*. Paris: Payot. Eng. *Course in General Linguistics*. Glasgow 1974: Fontana/Collins.

Schilder, P. (1923): *Das Körperschema; Ein Beitrag zur Lehre vom Bewusstsein des eigenen Körpers*. Berlin: Springer.

Searles, H. F. (1976): *Psychoanalytic Therapy with Schizophrenic Patients in a Private-Practice Context*. In: *Counter-transference and Related Subjects*. New York 1979: International Universities Press: 582–602.

Segal, H. (1975): "Psycho-Analytic Approach to the Treatment of Schizophrenia." *British Journal of Psychiatry*. Special Publication no. 10: 94–97.

Smith, J. Chr. (1946): *Psykiatriske Forelaesninger*. Copenhagen: Munksgaard.

Tausk, V. (1919): *Über die Entstehung des "Beeinflussungsapparates" in der Schizophrenie*. Zeitschrift für ärtzliche Psychoanalyse, no. 5: 1–33. Eng. "On the Origin of the 'Influencing Machine' in Schizophrenia." *Psychoanalytic Quarterly*, no. 2: 519–556.

Wulff, E. (1972): *Psychiatrie und Klassengesellschaft*. Frankfurt am Main: Fischer Verlag.

Wunderlich, D. (1971): *Pragmatik, Sprechsituation, Deixis. Zeitschrift für Literaturwissenschaft und Linguistik*, Heft 1–2.

INDEX